"Ethan's passion for fresh and delicious food has been a staple at his restaurants for years, and the craftsmanship in his dishes is a testament to his drive for serving soulfully inspired foods. Now the world can take a glimpse into the mind and recipes that have set Ethan apart from the rest."

—CHRIS COSENTINO, executive chef of Incanto

"Ethan Stowell is a northwestern jewel in every epicurean sense of the word. His influence on the Seattle food scene is unmistakable, and his personal take on Italian food is at once sophisticated yet simple and understated—a delectable combination. I appreciate Ethan's intrinsic wine savvy; his food seamlessly matches at the table, creating memorable and delicious pairings."

—EVAN GOLDSTEIN, author of *Perfect Pairings* and *Daring Pairings*

Ethan Stowell's
New Italian Kitchen

Bold Cooking from Seattle's
Anchovies & Olives, How to Cook a Wolf,
Staple & Fancy Mercantile, and Tavolàta

Ethan Stowell and Leslie Miller

Photography by Geoffrey Smith

TEN SPEED PRESS
Berkeley

Published in the United States by Ten Speed Press, an imprint of the Crown Publishing Group, a division of Random House, Inc., New York.
www.crownpublishing.com
www.tenspeed.com

Ten Speed Press and the Ten Speed Press colophon are registered trademarks of Random House, Inc.

Library of Congress Cataloging-in-Publication Data
Stowell, Ethan.
 Ethan Stowell's new Italian : bold cooking from the Pacific Northwest / Ethan Stowell and Leslie Miller. — 1st ed.
   p. cm.
 Includes index.
 Summary: "The debut cookbook from Seattle's acclaimed young chef, Ethan Stowell, chef/owner of Union, Tavolata, How to Cook a Wolf, and Anchovies & Olives, featuring refined yet unfussy modern-Italian cooking that showcases the best of Pacific Northwest ingredients"—Provided by publisher.
 1. Cookery, Italian. 2. Cookery—Washington—Seattle. I. Miller, Leslie (Leslie Ann) II. Title.
 TX723.S7986 2010
 641.5945—dc22

                                        2010016234
ISBN 978-1-58008-818-3

Printed in China
Design by Nancy Austin
10 9 8 7 6 5 4 3 2 1
First Edition

Contents

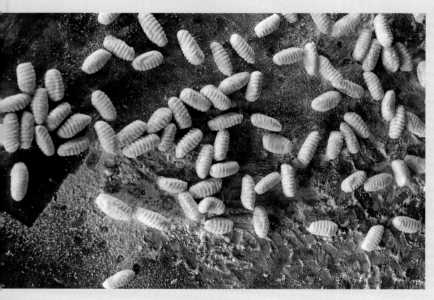

Beasties of the Land . . .

. . . and Sea

Cheese for the Civilized and Desserts for the Rest of You

Building Blocks: Condiments, Sauces, and Staples

Acknowledgments

I owe everything to my dog, Cleo (see picture below—cute, huh?) After Cleo, there are probably a few people I should thank, starting with my wife, Angela, who helps me keep everything in perspective. I love you. I would like to thank my mother and my father, who set great examples for me growing up and would probably agree that I'm not quite there yet, and my brothers who show me that the hours and work I put in aren't much by comparison.

There are so many amazingly talented people that I work with that I can only say you inspire me and make me look good on a daily basis. Thank you. Eli Dahlin, who helped create the wonderful desserts contained in this book, and Union and its crew that gave me my start have my deepest appreciation. Many thanks to Old John, who taught me a lot and helped me grow up. Though if you don't stop using so much salt I won't come over for dinner anymore.

To Aaron, Melissa, and the rest of the Ten Speed crew, thank you for being incredible to work with and making this book happen. Geoff, you took the book to another level with fabulous photographs.

Kirsten Graham, my publicist, knows I'm not always pleasant to work with and getting recipes back on time is not my strength. Thank you for putting up with me since the beginning and saving my ass time and again. For Lam, my co-writer, it has been a distinct pleasure getting to know you and work with you. Hopefully this is just the start of many projects together.

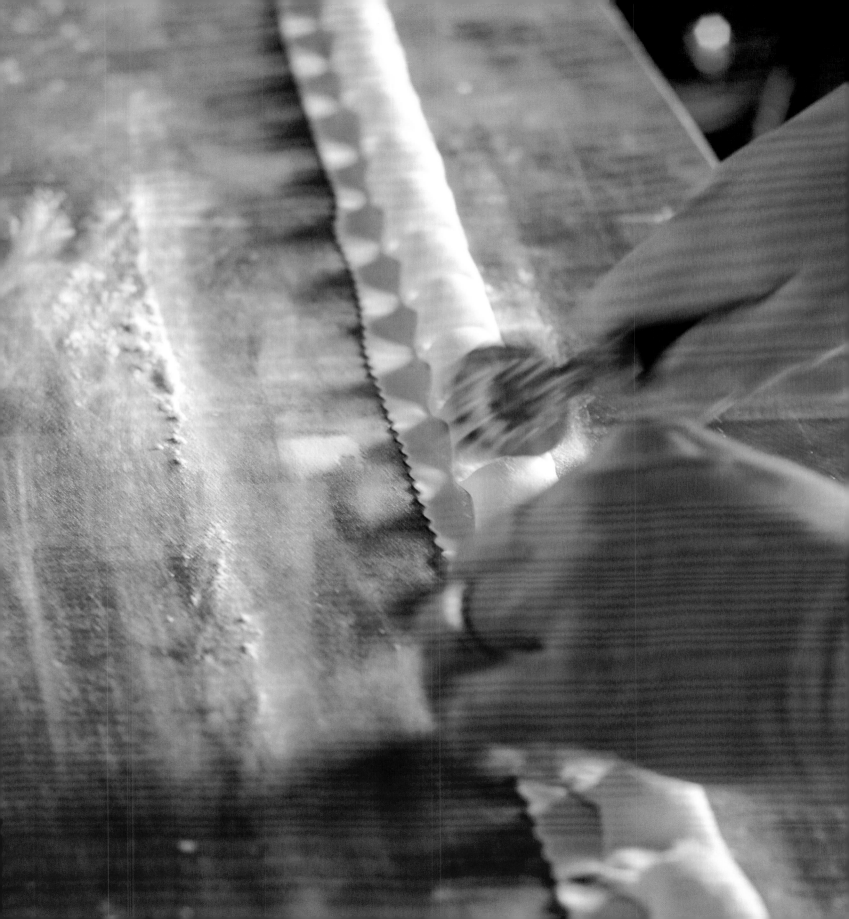

Introduction

Okay, this is my ideal dinner. There are two of you—cozy, but not alone. Laughter and music float around you, as does the muted percussion of silver on porcelain. There's that soft light that makes everyone look better and a bottle of wine on the table. It doesn't have to be pricey, just good. Out come a series of plates, not too small, not too big, but shareable. I'm not talking about doling out little bits onto dainty saucers—more like a bowl of handmade pasta set down between you with two forks sticking out of the steam. Or maybe it's an impeccably fresh crudo, the ocean flavors clean and bright, that preps you for the grilled zucchini salad, or maybe a tangle of white beans and grilled shrimp. What follows is a perfectly roasted quail or fresh branzino you unapologetically suck off the bones.

The goal is a series of tastes. Each of you gets to try a little bit of everything, eating just enough of each dish so you feel sated, but not so much that it dulls your enthusiasm for the next dish issuing from the kitchen, whether that's a soft-boiled egg with anchovy mayonnaise or beef carpaccio or maybe some orecchiette with grilled octopus and Taggiasca olives. This is the way I cook in my restaurants, and this is the way I eat. This is the way I hope you will eat, too.

When I opened each of my Seattle restaurants, I tried for places that were sexy without being slick; I wanted intimate spaces that glow with soft wood and copper, or that gather strangers at a thick communal table, *la tavolàta*. Overall, I wanted to reinforce the idea that food shouldn't be formal or fussy, just focused. And, more than that, that eating is an art more walk-up than doorman, more warehouse than gallery. It's got to be good, but it's also got to be fun.

You'll find very few lengthy ingredient lists inside this book, no foams or caul-fat wrappers or four-page spreads. You will find recipes meant to be both modern and seductive, every recipe designed for a shareable meal that would be at place at my ideal dinner table. I'd like you to think just as much about the method as the meals, and make different choices about not only what you eat, but how you eat. Instead of doubling the recipes for bigger parties and families, I'd like you to consider adding another dish or two instead, allowing each of your guests even more delectable forkfuls, scoops, nibbles, and tastes. There is joy and abundance inherent in thoughtful food done right—you don't need to douse it with truffle oil to make food special. Incredible, pristine ingredients suffer from being overly dolled up, but if there were no magic in how we put ingredients together, then I'd be out of a job. Let's get back not to the food we used to eat—this isn't nonna's Italian—but to a more time-tested philosophy of *how* we eat, allowing us to create and share food at its best, eating the way we were meant to, with each other.

It was during my first stint in a restaurant kitchen—there among the misfits and mad geniuses, most of them unfit for human company and therefore well suited to restaurant hours—that I felt, for the first time, like I was truly among my people. I worked my way up the line, tasting and learning along the way from people with incredible skills and artistry. In those first jobs I did very precise French cooking, the type of cooking that I, and many others, thought to be the height of culinary artistry. I'm still glad for those years; they taught me incredible focus and important skills in prep and plating. But it was with Italian-inflected cuisine that I felt the same jolt that I did during my first restaurant job. I fell in love, not only with the food itself—fresh, rustic—but also with the philosophy behind the food. Everything seemed meant to share, meant to inspire joy and fun. It was food that was meant to feed the spirit as much as the body.

And that is how I shape my idea of how a meal should go. The arc of the meal should build in terms of weight, body, flavor, and texture instead of building up the portion size. That is why you won't find the recipes in this book organized according to a traditional layout: appetizers, pastas, entrées, and desserts. In place of that traditional framework, the book organizes recipes into broad categories so that you can customize the dishes and build the flavor in your own perfect meal. Along with the arc of flavor, I recommend employing a little common sense; if you are serving a heavier or more elaborate meat dish, for example, don't preface it with three courses. You want people to feel happy and satisfied, not stuffed.

Just like a dinner guest, I want you to read this book and feel happy and satisfied, inspired but not overwhelmed. Like you, I love cookbooks; I own more than a few myself. For years, after every shift, I pored through recipes, a certain few cookbooks at my bedside. It's that cookbook—the one you read at night like a novel, the one that inspires you but doesn't take itself too seriously—that I endeavored to write for you. I consider it a privilege to make food for people, and I make an effort to do it with enthusiasm and imagination every time I step into the kitchen. If you take that attitude with you into your own kitchen (and maybe this book, too), it's pretty hard to go wrong.

A Note on Ingredients

The recipes in this book are straightforward and depend not only on technique but also on using the very best ingredients you can find and afford. If you are too tight on time to make your own pasta or are making a dish that calls for dried, go to an Italian grocery that sells and imports artisanal brands. While you are there, buy the best extra-virgin olive oil you can find—you'll use it with abandon when you prepare these recipes.

- Use only kosher salt, unless a finishing salt such as fleur de sel is specified. Grind your pepper fresh from the mill.
- If your tap water isn't perfect, use springwater for the recipes; this is especially important for preparing soups.
- Make sure your eggs are fresh and preferably buy them from the farmers' market; likewise with your fruits and vegetables. You'll be delighted by the results if you let the seasons and availability guide your choices.

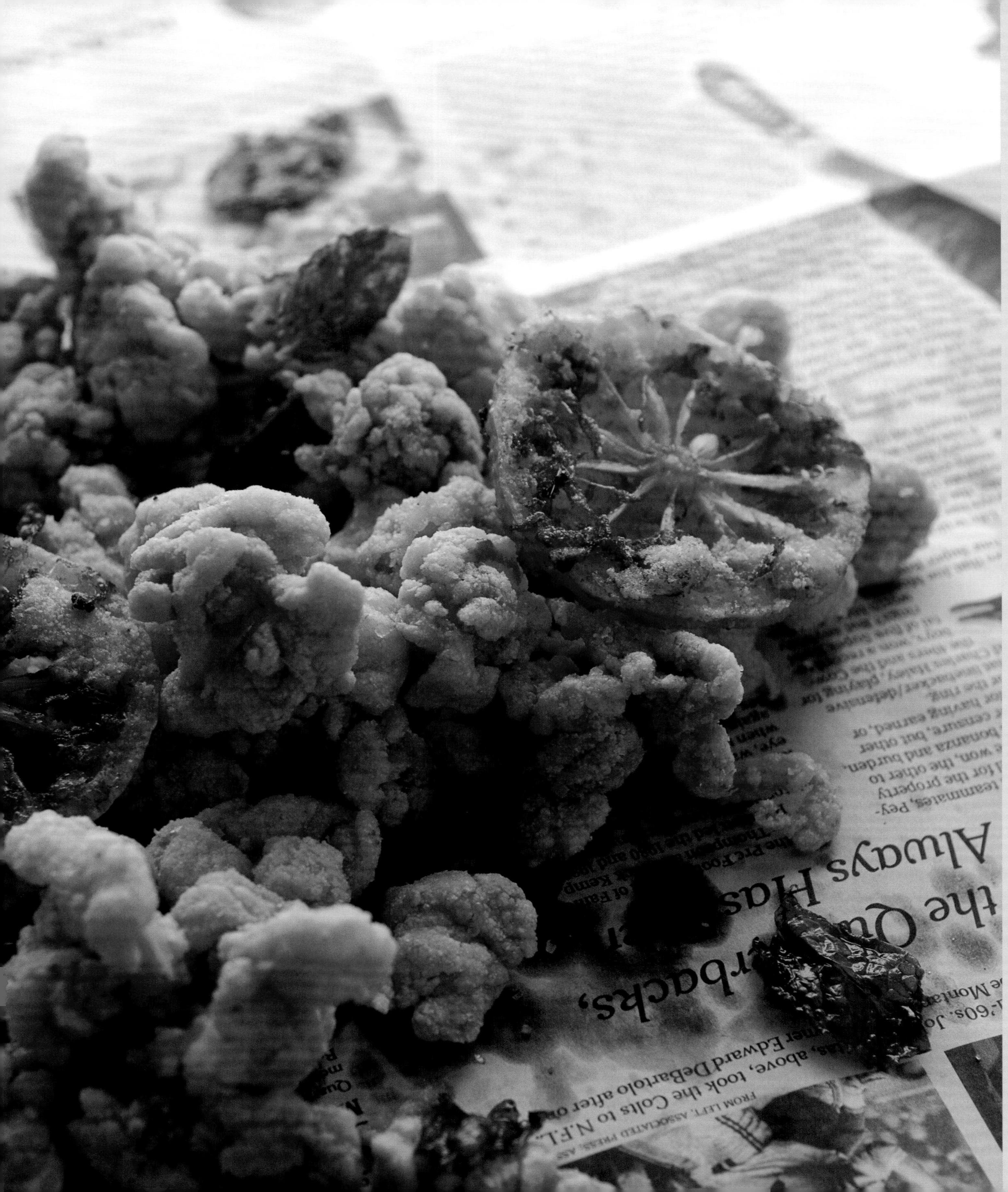

Nibbles and Bits

Mixing and matching dishes from this section is a wonderful way to eat, whether it's two of you or six or eight. Creating a meal out of these plates lets you use smaller amounts of ingredients and gives your guests or family small flavor bursts. You probably don't want to eat a whole plate of crudo, but sharing the Spot Prawn Crudo, nibbling on marinated baby vegetables, or having a bite or two of a Soft-Shell Crab Bruschetta—I don't know anyone who would turn down starting, or doing—a meal this way.

The crudos, simply Italian for "raw," honor the ingredients by showcasing their inherent taste and texture. Whether it's beef or escolar, I like to slice it in such a way that it has a little bite to it. To me, there is something critical that is lost when you slice all raw ingredients paper-thin; a large part of the enjoyment comes from the feel of the meat or fish on your tongue, between your teeth. Especially because of the wealth of incredible fish and seafood in Seattle, crudos are becoming increasingly popular. Diners also realize that crudos make simple and elegant starters, and that the preparation speaks to the respect the cook has for the ingredients on the plate. Think of the recipes that follow as guidelines; as you get more comfortable, you will know that you can swap out spot prawns for swordfish and create a dish with a totally new taste and texture. Use different oils, fruits, and chiles to bring out the fish's best characteristics without covering up anything.

As much as I love crudos, I would never say no to a paper cone of fried clams with a side of aioli for dipping. They're in here, the aioli brightened up with sorrel, as are Fried Artichokes Pangratatto and Crispy Young Favas, too. I have no truck with those snobby chefs who think that a fryer has no place in the modern kitchen or think it's trashy. People like fried things. It's a good day when you get past worrying about your reputation and start prioritizing making food people love, and that includes fresh bowls of pasta and fried oysters, too. If you're worried about being judged for making that kind of comfort food as a chef, then you got into the biz for the wrong reason. Chefs should cook for the same reason you do—because you enjoy making beautiful food for people.

Baked Stellar Bay Kusshi Oysters with Garlic Breadcrumbs and Oregano

I love broiling Kusshis not only because they have a lovely, delicate texture and a good brininess, but also because they have deeply cupped shells that hold both liquid and a lot of delicious breadcrumbs. Cherrystone clams would be a great substitute, and Totten Virginica, Barron Point, or Shigoku oysters would also work well, because they are the right size to hold up to the heat. Save tiny Kumomotos for eating on the half shell.

1/4 cup Garlic Breadcrumbs (page 220)

3 cloves garlic, very finely chopped

3 heaping tablespoons finely chopped fresh parsley

1 tablespoon chopped fresh oregano

Grated zest of 1 lemon

1 teaspoon kosher salt

Freshly cracked pepper

24 Kusshi oysters

Rock salt

Juice of 2 lemons

Extra-virgin olive oil

Preheat the broiler on the lowest setting.

Combine the breadcrumbs with the garlic, parsley, oregano, lemon zest, kosher salt, and a few grinds of pepper.

Shuck the oysters over a bowl to catch the liquor. Discard the top shells. Put an inch or so of rock salt in a baking dish large enough to hold the shells. Stabilize the bottom shells in the rock salt and return the shucked oysters to their shells.

Strain the reserved oyster liquor through a fine-mesh strainer and add the lemon juice. Divide the liquid among the oysters.

Sprinkle the oysters very liberally with the breadcrumb mixture and drizzle lightly with olive oil. Broil for 4 to 5 minutes, or until the breadcrumbs are golden brown and crispy. Serve immediately.

Bruschetta with Smashed Chickpeas and Grilled Lamb's Tongue

Tongues have an awesome richness that goes completely underappreciated because people don't serve them, fearing a food that can taste them. That's silly. Tongues are cheap and delicious, and enjoyment of this unique cut is all in the preparation. Once I found a reliable tongue source, I was elated, and I started putting them on the restaurant menus in an attempt to win more converts. For this dish, the meat does need a while to cook, but you can poach them up to a day in advance.

GRILLED LAMB'S TONGUES

3 stalks celery, cut into thirds

1 head garlic, cut in half horizontally

1 onion, peeled and halved

2 large carrots, peeled and halved

2 fresh bay leaves

1 teaspoon peppercorns

4 fresh lamb's tongues

SMASHED CHICKPEAS

2 cups Basic Chickpeas (page 220)

1/4 cup chickpea-cooking liquid

1/4 cup extra-virgin olive oil

Kosher salt and freshly ground pepper

BRUSCHETTA

1 baguette

Extra-virgin olive oil, for brushing

Kosher salt and freshly ground pepper

Aged balsamic vinegar

To prepare the lamb's tongues, place all the ingredients in a deep pot and cover with 2 inches of water. Bring to a boil over high heat, then lower the heat to maintain a simmer. Place a heatproof plate in the pot to weight down the tongues and ensure they cook evenly. Cook the tongues for about 3 hours, maintaining a bare simmer. Skim off the scum occasionally and top off the water level as needed. The tongues are done when the skin pulls off easily.

Remove the tongues from the liquid and allow to cool just long enough so you can handle them. Peel the skin from the tongues, then remove all the fat, gristle, and bone. Split each tongue in half lengthwise.

To make the smashed chickpeas, place the chickpeas in a food processor along with the cooking liquid. Pulse until combined. Add the oil in a steady stream. Season to taste with salt and pepper. Set aside at room temperature.

To make the bruschetta, cut 4 slices from the baguette on the diagonal, 1 to 1 1/2 inches thick. Brush generously on both sides with olive oil and sprinkle with salt. Grill on both sides to mark or use a panini press to toast and crisp the bread.

When ready to serve, season the tongues on both sides with salt and pepper and drizzle with olive oil. Using a panini press or a grill, cook to heat through and mark on both sides.

Spread the chickpea purée on the baguette toasts, top with the grilled tongues, then drizzle each with the aged balsamic vinegar. Serve immediately.

Crispy Young Favas with Green Garlic Mayonnaise

This cooking method only works with the very first favas of spring—the ones that are thin skinned enough to be eaten whole. Not only is this a light, crunchy, and addictive snack, but it's also a nice way to enjoy fava beans without all the fuss. For dipping, mild green garlic makes for an aioli that doesn't overwhelm the favas' sweet flavor.

1 cup sifted cornmeal

3 cups sifted all-purpose flour

Kosher salt and freshly ground pepper

1 pound fava beans, stems removed

1 cup milk

Canola oil, for frying

Green Garlic Mayonnaise (recipe follows)

Sift the cornmeal and flour together to combine. Season with salt and pepper. Dip the favas into the milk, then coat in the flour/cornmeal mixture.

Fill a large, heavy pot or Dutch oven with canola oil to a depth of 3 inches and heat to 350°F. Fry the fava beans in batches for about 3 minutes, or until golden brown. Remove to a bowl lined with paper towels to absorb the excess oil and add salt immediately. Serve with the mayo for dipping.

GREEN GARLIC MAYONNAISE

1 fresh egg yolk

3 tablespoons water

1 teaspoon Dijon mustard

Juice of 1 lemon

1 stalk green garlic, bulb and stem sliced

$1^1/_2$ cups canola oil

Kosher salt

Place the yolk, water, mustard, lemon juice, and garlic in a food processor. Pulse to combine. With the motor running, add the oil in a slow, steady stream. Season to taste with salt. If the mayo seems too thick for dipping, thin with a little extra water.

Beef Carpaccio with Preserved Pecorino Sardo and Arugula

Two things you should know about me and carpaccio: First, I don't like carpaccio you can see through; I cut mine a little thicker, which gives it better texture and body. Second, I like my carpaccio loaded, the way some people think of nachos or pizza. Here I use some *bococcini de pecorino* that we keep in the restaurants and some tender baby arugula, but you could use shaved porcini mushrooms, shaved raw artichokes, or sautéed chanterelles—whatever you like. Just load it up.

1 pound beef tenderloin

8 ounces baby arugula

1 tablespoon extra-virgin olive oil

2 teaspoons fresh lemon juice

Kosher salt and freshly cracked pepper

4 ounces Preserved Pecorino Sardo (page 218), plus 1 tablespoon marinating oil

Trim the tenderloin of all visible fat and sinew. Wrap tightly in plastic and then place in the freezer for at least 2 hours, preferably overnight.

Pick the most tender and succulent tips from the arugula and place in a bowl. Toss with the olive oil and 1 teaspoon of the lemon juice.

Remove the tenderloin from the freezer and unwrap the plastic. Using your sharpest knife, slice the meat into $1/4$-inch coins. Arrange the meat on a large platter in overlapping slices. Season generously with salt and cracked pepper. Dot the meat with the preserved pecorino and drizzle the marinating oil over all. Sprinkle with the remaining 1 teaspoon lemon juice. Mound the arugula in the center of the plate and serve.

Carne Cruda with Anchovy and Garlic

Some people will tell you that it's okay to make carne cruda, known as "steak tartare" in fancy French circles, in a food processor. Sorry, no go. You don't chop it, pulse it, or otherwise mangle it. You freeze it, slice it, crosscut it, and dice it. Period. Yes, chopping the meat by hand requires patience, but it creates the perfect texture. Freezing the meat beforehand makes this job easier. This is one of those recipes where you must use the very best ingredients you can find—the best olive oil, the best imported anchovies—to take this crudo over the top. Buy the best New York strip or tenderloin you can afford, and tell your butcher how you're serving the meat to ensure you get the very best. For a light meal, serve with plenty of crusty bread and a small salad.

12 ounces trimmed New York strip or tenderloin

3 cloves Preserved Garlic (page 217)

4 anchovy fillets

1/2 lemon

3 tablespoons extra-virgin olive oil

1 tablespoon water

Kosher salt and freshly cracked black pepper

Using a sharp knife, go over the meat one more time to ensure all excess fat and sinew have been removed. Wrap the meat tightly in plastic and freeze overnight.

Mash the garlic with the flat side of a chef's knife, then chop until puréed and put into a bowl. Chop the anchovy fillets very finely and add to the garlic. Using a grater, zest the lemon into the bowl. Add the olive oil and stir to blend.

Remove the meat from the freezer and unwrap. Using your sharpest knife, slice the meat into 1/4-inch slices, then crosscut the slices into 1/4-inch strips. Cut across the strips to form a fine dice.

Add the meat to the bowl along with the water to help smooth out the mixture and make it a little less rich. Toss gently. Season to taste with salt and pepper and serve.

VARIATION: TAKE IT OLD-SCHOOL

Instead of plating the carne cruda individually, pile it elegantly on a plate and make a shallow depression in the center. Separate an impeccably fresh egg and gently place the yolk in the well.

Fried Artichokes Pangratatto

The only way to improve upon a fried artichoke is to shower it with fried-garlic breadcrumbs, making a hands-on dish a little bit messier and a lot tastier. This is a great little antipasto, excellent with a light white wine or served with cold beer for a ballgame snack that ranks more than a few steps above nachos. Eat the larger leaves just as you would if you had a bowl of melted butter sitting right there, scraping the leaves against your teeth. The tender stems and inner leaves can be eaten whole.

Canola oil, for frying

1 lemon

1/2 cup Garlic Breadcrumbs (page 220)

1 tablespoon chopped fresh oregano

1 tablespoon chopped fresh parsley

2 large artichokes

Kosher salt

Extra-virgin olive oil, for drizzling

Fill a deep, heavy pot or Dutch oven with 3 inches of canola oil and heat to 350°F.

While the oil is heating, zest the lemon using a grater. Cut the lemon in half, squeeze the juice into a bowl, and set aside. Combine the breadcrumbs, oregano, lemon zest, and parsley in a bowl and set aside.

To prepare the artichokes, first peel the fibrous outer covering from the stems, trimming only the very bottom and leaving as much stem intact as possible. (See step-by-step photos on pages 16 and 17.) Cut off the top of each artichoke with a very sharp chef's knife. Next, pull off all the tough outer leaves. Use kitchen shears to snip off the tops of the tender inner leaves. Quarter the artichoke and remove the choke from each quarter. Brush the cut surfaces of the artichoke quarters with the reserved lemon juice to prevent discoloration.

When ready to fry, pat the artichokes completely dry. Fry in batches for 3 to 4 minutes, or until lightly browned and crispy and the stems are tender when pierced with a knife.

Drain on paper towels and season with salt while hot. Place in a shallow bowl and drizzle lightly with the olive oil, then sprinkle with the seasoned breadcrumbs. Serve immediately.

Fried Ipswich Clams with Sorrel Aioli

This dish channels the best of the clam shacks that dot the East Coast. Here, a crunchy cornmeal coating and a quick dip in hot oil render these soft-shell clams succulent and juicy. As an accompaniment, chopped sorrel gives aioli a lemony lift and gorgeous color for a nice twist on tartar sauce. For fun, serve them to your guests the way we do in the restaurants—in little paper cones. They're not hard to fold, make for great oil-absorbing containers, and make you feel like you're on the boardwalk.

Canola oil, for frying

1 1/2 cups sifted all-purpose flour

1/2 cup sifted cornmeal

Kosher salt and freshly ground pepper

24 freshly shucked soft-shell clams

1 cup milk

Sorrel Aioli (recipe follows)

Fill a deep, heavy pot with 3 inches of canola oil and heat to 350°F.

Combine the flour and cornmeal on a shallow plate and season with salt and pepper. Dip each clam into the milk, then dredge in the flour mixture.

Fry the clams in batches until golden brown, about 4 minutes. Remove to a paper towel–lined plate and season with salt while hot. Serve with the aioli for dipping.

SORREL AIOLI

1 fresh egg yolk

2 tablespoons water

1 teaspoon Dijon mustard

Juice of 1/2 lemon

10 sorrel leaves, chopped

1 1/2 cups canola oil

Kosher salt

Place the egg yolk, water, mustard, lemon juice, and sorrel in a food processor. Pulse a few times to combine. With the motor running, add the oil in a slow, steady stream. Season to taste with salt.

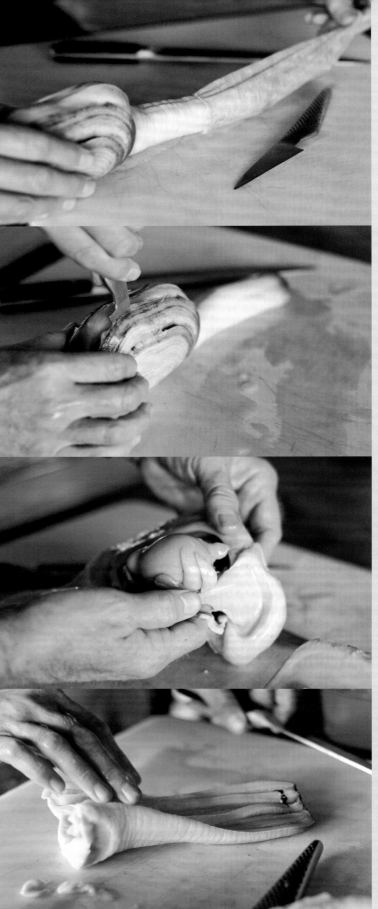

Fun with Geoduck

Most of us reared on the West Coast are well acquainted with the rather unattractive and frankly suggestive bivalve known as the geoduck (pronounced *gooey-duck*), or the giant clam. Although they may be ugly and require a bit of prep, geoducks are unbelievably sweet and succulent.

The meat from the siphon—the long dangling bit—is best served raw and makes fabulous ceviches and crudos. The mantle—the part found inside the shell of the clam—holds up well to cooking, and in the recipe on page 24, I've folded it into some creamy scrambled eggs, made even richer with the addition of crème fraîche.

Allow the geoduck to relax for at least 30 minutes, resting the shell on the lip of the sink with the siphon hanging down. This allows the siphon to soften and elongate. While the geoduck is resting, bring a pot of water to a boil and prepare an ice-water bath. After it has rested, plunge the entire geoduck into the boiling water for no more than 30 seconds and immediately shock in the ice water. This step is necessary for removal of the tough skin encasing the siphon.

Once the clam has cooled, peel off the shell, being very careful not to cut yourself. Grab the loose skin around the siphon at the base and pull down, peeling the skin off as you go.

Next, pull off the ball-like intestinal sac that rests below the mantle at the base of the siphon. Remove any darker colored bits that don't come off with the sac and discard.

You should be left with the mantle and the siphon. Although the flesh of the siphon will toughen with cooking and is best served raw, the mantle can hold up to some heat. Separate the two pieces by cutting off the siphon at the base, right where the flesh turns from white to ivory. Slice the siphon in half lengthwise and rinse under running water to remove any lingering sand. Split the mantle in half and slice it very thinly.

Geoduck Crudo with Fennel and Radish

In this fabulous crudo, baby fennel and radish offset the sweetness of the geoduck. This dish has an especially lovely texture to it, with the silken geoduck intermingling with the shaved vegetables. Serve with crusty bread to soak up all the goodness.

1 prepped geoduck siphon (see page 23), halved lengthwise and sliced paper-thin

Juice of 2 limes

4 Easter egg radishes, shaved with a mandoline

3 baby fennel, shaved with a mandoline

1 jalapeño chile, seeded and minced

1/4 cup extra-virgin olive oil

Kosher salt and freshly cracked black pepper

Combine the geoduck, lime juice, radishes, fennel, chile, and olive oil in a large bowl and toss gently. Season to taste with salt and pepper. Divide among 4 plates and drizzle the remaining juice over each portion.

Geoduck Scramble with Crème Fraîche

This would make a lovely brunch dish, but you could serve it as an appetizer, too, with some toasted or grilled bread and a glass of sparkling. The quenelle of crème fraîche is made using two spoons like paddles to shape softer ingredients into an oval or a football. For a throwback to dot.com excess, pile some caviar on top if you like. If you aren't feeling fancy, just dollop the crème fraîche on top instead.

3 tablespoons unsalted butter

8 fresh eggs

Kosher salt and freshly ground pepper

1 prepped geoduck mantle (see page 23), halved and thinly sliced

3 tablespoons minced chives

4 tablespoons crème fraîche

Melt the butter in a sauté pan over medium heat. Crack the eggs into a bowl, season with salt and pepper, and beat lightly. Add the geoduck mantle to the beaten eggs and stir to combine. Pour the mixture into the prepared pan and scramble, over medium to low heat, until the eggs are creamy and just set. Add the chives and stir.

Divide among 4 shallow bowls and top each with a quenelle of crème fraîche.

Manila Clams on the Half Shell with Fennel, Lemon, and Chiles

If you love fried clams or a nice bowl of clam chowder, then eating clams on the half shell will be a revelation for you. Serving clams as a crudo plays up their assertive, concentrated clam flavor and guarantees tender meat. It's easy, delicious, and a little bit different. If you don't have baby fennel, you can use finely chopped fennel bulb. For a less spicy dish, you can split the chile lengthwise and remove the seeds and membrane first, then dice.

1 cup thinly sliced baby fennel

Juice of 2 lemons

$1/4$ cup best-quality olive oil

1 serrano chile, sliced crosswise paper-thin

24 Manila clams

Combine the fennel, lemon juice, oil, and chile in a small bowl and let marinate for 10 minutes or so while you shuck the clams.

Shucking clams is a little different from shucking oysters. You can do it from the hinge with an oyster knife, or you can get a clam knife and go in from the lip side. If you're going to do it, ask your fishmonger, very sweetly, whether he or she will demonstrate the technique for you if you've never done it before. The clam knife has a thin blade and slides through the lip with the flat side, not the tip.

Place the shucked clams on a large plate. Pile the fennel mixture high on each clam, spooning some of the liquid over the top of each one. Serve immediately.

Sardine Crudo with Celery Hearts, Pine Nuts, and Lemon

If you simply can't get past the idea that sardines are oily and fishy, let this crudo change your mind. The key to this dish is using sweet celery hearts—the tender, yellow, innermost bits of the head. You might think of this as the part of the celery that goes in the compost pile, but the truth is that the small yellow leaves have incredible flavor, and the pale stalks add texture without strings. As with all crudos, use your very best olive oil.

8 fresh sardines

1 lemon

3 center ribs celery with leaves

Kosher salt and freshly ground pepper

5 tablespoons extra-virgin olive oil

2 tablespoons pine nuts

To prepare the fish, lay out a sardine on your cutting board and begin by cutting off the head, or simply pull it off by bending it back and tugging. Next, using a small, sharp knife, cut a slit down the belly and remove and discard the innards. Gently pry open the sardine to butterfly the fish and lay it flat like a book. Run your fingers along and underneath the backbone, beginning with the head and moving toward the tail. Loosen the backbone and ribs from the flesh and lift, taking out the tail with the bones. Remove any stray bones with tweezers and cut the fillet in half lengthwise. Repeat with the remaining fish.

Lay the lemon on its side and cut a slice off the top and bottom of the fruit, then stand it on a flat end. Using a sharp knife and following the curve of the fruit, slice down the sides of the lemon, removing all the peel and pith to reveal the fruit. Once the peel and pith are removed, hold the lemon in your palm. Cut along the membrane on each side of the individual sections and allow the flesh to fall into a bowl. When the lemon is sectioned, coarsely chop the flesh and return to the bowl. Squeeze the remaining membrane into the bowl to catch all the lemon juice. Set aside.

Pinch off the leaves from the celery ribs and place in a bowl. You should end up with about $^{1}/_{4}$ cup of celery leaves in all. Slice the ribs very thinly crosswise and add to the leaves. Season with salt and toss with 1 tablespoon of the olive oil. Add the pine nuts and toss.

To serve, place 4 fillets, skin side up, on each of 4 plates. Drizzle each serving with 1 tablespoon of the remaining olive oil and season with salt and pepper. Divide the lemon and juice among the plates, spooning them on top of the fillets. Finally, top each with one-fourth of the celery and pine nut salad. Serve immediately.

Marinated Octopus

SERVES 8

Italians say that to ensure your octopus is tender, first you pound it on the dock as you bring it in from the boat, then you put a cork in the cooking pot. I don't know what magical alchemic properties are supposed to be at work there, but I always put a cork in my pot, just to be sure. I like to use bigger octopi because I think they have more developed flavor. They're a little chewier, but I don't mind—that's just part of the joy of octopus. Use the recipe as a guideline, and feel free to experiment with combinations of whatever aromatics you have on hand. As a variation, add 2 cups cooked corona beans to the octopus as it marinates.

1 (8-pound) octopus, cleaned

1 cork (see headnote)

1 tablespoon peppercorns

2 carrots, peeled

1 onion, halved

1 head garlic, halved

1 bulb fennel, halved

2 ribs celery, halved

3 fresh or 2 dried bay leaves

Kosher salt and freshly ground pepper

1/4 cup fresh lemon juice

3/4 cup extra-virgin olive oil

1 or 2 lemons (enough to produce 1/4 cup juice)

1 orange

1 shallot

1 clove garlic, sliced paper-thin

Generous pinch of chile flakes

In a large stockpot, place the octopus, cork, peppercorns, carrots, onion, garlic head, fennel, celery, and bay leaves. Cover with cold water. Bring to a light boil and then keep at the barest simmer for 1 hour to 1 hour and 15 minutes, or until the octopus is tender. Place the entire pot in the refrigerator and allow the octopus to cool in the liquid.

When cool, remove the octopus from the liquid, discarding the liquid. Cut into 1-inch chunks, including the head. Sprinkle with salt and pepper.

In a large bowl, combine the lemon juice and olive oil. Using a vegetable peeler, remove the zest from the lemon(s) and orange in large strips and add to the bowl. Slice the shallot into rings and add to the bowl with the sliced garlic and chile flakes. Add the octopus chunks and toss to coat. Allow to marinate at room temperature for about 1 hour, stirring about every 10 minutes to mingle the flavors. Serve at room temperature.

Pickled Vegetables

SERVES 4

These quick pickles make nice nibbles with drinks, and are great served with charcuterie. You can vary the vegetables according to what looks best in the market—just make sure they are fresh and attractive and that you cut them into roughly the same size so they become tender at the same time.

1/8 cup kosher salt

1/4 cup sugar

3 cups red wine vinegar

3 cups water

2 tablespoons black peppercorns

1 tablespoon coriander seeds

1 tablespoon mustard seeds

3 fresh bay leaves

6 to 8 cloves garlic, halved lengthwise

10 ounces pearl onions, peeled, trimmed, and halved lengthwise

1 bunch baby beets, trimmed and cut into eighths

1 head cauliflower, broken into tiny florets

1 bunch baby carrots, peeled, trimmed, and halved lengthwise

1 bunch radishes, trimmed and quartered

3 red jalapeño chiles, sliced thickly crosswise

In a large pot, combine the salt, sugar, vinegar, water, peppercorns, coriander seeds, mustard seeds, bay leaves, garlic, and onions. Place over high heat and bring to a boil, stirring occasionally. When the mixture reaches a rolling boil, add the beets, cauliflower, carrots, radishes, and chiles and remove from the heat.

Once the mixture has cooled to room temperature, transfer the vegetables and brine to a nonreactive container and chill. The vegetables will keep for 1 to 2 weeks refrigerated in a tightly covered container.

Nibbles and Bits　　　**29**

Sea Bass Crudo with Vanilla Oil, English Peas, and Mint

Using vanilla in savory dishes has become more popular, but don't discount it as just a fad. The vanilla adds a depth and a fragrance that your guests probably won't be able to peg right off the bat, but I guarantee they'll love the combination. Sea bass has a clean, slightly buttery flavor that really works with the vanilla oil, while the peas add sweetness and texture and the mint brightens the whole thing up.

The extra vanilla oil will last up to 2 weeks in the fridge, and makes a fabulous addition to vinaigrettes. Save the vanilla pod and bury it in sugar, or cover it in vodka to make your own extract.

$1/2$ vanilla bean

$1/2$ cup best-quality extra-virgin olive oil

$3/4$-pound piece sea bass

Kosher salt

$1/4$ pound English peas, blanched

3 fresh mint leaves

$1/2$ lemon

To make the vanilla oil, split the bean lengthwise and, using the flat edge of a knife, scrape the seeds from the inside. Combine the seeds with the olive oil in a small squeeze bottle and shake vigorously.

Slice the sea bass into $1/4$-inch slices; each person should have about 3 ounces of fish.

Rub the bottoms of 4 shallow bowls with a bit of the vanilla oil. Arrange the fish on top in a single layer. Sprinkle with salt. Scatter the peas evenly over the fish.

Roll the mint leaves into a tight cigar shape and cut into a chiffonade. Sprinkle the mint over the peas and fish. Drizzle each with vanilla oil and squeeze about 1 teaspoon lemon juice over each. Serve immediately.

Soft-Shell Crab Bruschetta with Spring Garlic Aioli

Not an authentic bruschetta (you'd never eat this dish in Italy), this appetizer is damn good all the same, with the garlicky aioli making a rich bed for the crispy grilled crabs. Look for soft-shell crabs in May through July, when blue crabs begin to molt and shed their hard shells. Once they do, it takes about four days for their new shells to solidify, and it's during this window that they are perfect for eating whole. It's best to buy soft-shell crabs live and kill and clean them yourself, but you may have them cleaned at the fishmonger and cook them as soon as possible once you get home.

4 (3- to 4-ounce) soft-shell crabs

4 thick-cut slices baguette

4 tablespoons extra-virgin olive oil, plus more for drizzling

Kosher salt and freshly ground pepper

2 cups loosely packed baby greens (such as arugula or watercress)

1 teaspoon fresh lemon juice

1 bulb spring onion, shaved with a mandoline

4 tablespoons Spring Garlic Aioli (page 217)

Rinse the live crabs under cold water. Using sharp scissors, cut off the head and white gills about $1/4$ inch behind the eyes. Next, bend back the thin piece that folds under the crab—called the apron—and twist until it breaks off, or cut off with scissors. The intestinal vein should come out at the same time. Rinse the crabs again and pat dry.

Heat a grill or grill pan on high. Brush the crabs and bread slices on both sides with 2 tablespoons of the olive oil. Sprinkle the crabs with salt and pepper. Grill the bread until browned and marked, about 1 minute per side. Grill the crabs until opaque and heated through, about 2 minutes per side.

Dress the greens with the remaining 2 tablespoons olive oil and the lemon juice, and season to taste with salt and pepper. Add the shaved onion and toss.

Sprinkle each toast with salt and top with a dollop of aioli. Divide the salad among the toasts and top each with a crab. Drizzle with olive oil and serve hot.

Spot Prawn Crudo with Chile and Mint

Spot prawns are actually shrimp, though they do sport four white spots on their shells, which makes the name at least partially accurate. By any name, these firm, sweet, and delicate aquatic beasties are a Pacific delicacy shown to their best advantage when served as a crudo and accented with clean flavors. If you can't find live spot prawns or other sashimi-grade shrimp, scallops, ahi, or albacore would all work nicely with the chile and mint. Wait to combine the chile, mint, and lime until you are ready to serve so that the lime juice doesn't "cook" the mint.

24 to 32 live spot prawns

Kosher salt and freshly cracked pepper

15 fresh mint leaves

2 limes

2 red jalapeño chiles

4 teaspoons best-quality extra-virgin olive oil, for drizzling

Remove the heads and shells from the prawns and clean them under cold running water. Pat dry and season with salt and pepper. Divide the prawns among 4 plates.

Roll the mint leaves into a cigar shape and slice thinly with a sharp knife. Place in a small, nonreactive bowl. With a grater, remove the zest from 1 of the limes and add to the mint leaves. Cut both limes in half and squeeze the juice into the bowl with the zest and mint. Seed and thinly slice or mince the chiles, depending on how much "bite" you want in the dish. Add to the bowl and toss to combine all the ingredients.

Spoon one-fourth of the mint-lime mixture over each portion of spot prawns. Drizzle each with 1 teaspoon of the olive oil and serve.

Frittata with Morels and Savory

Both winter and summer savory are related to the mint family, with a fairly strong flavor that rests somewhere between mint and thyme. Summer savory is a bit milder and makes a perfect partner to spring's first morels in this tasty frittata. This would make a nice light lunch served with a side salad and a glass of Italian white with enough texture to stand up to the frittata (I had a glass of 2007 Marco Felluga Friulano Bianco when we tested the recipe). Make sure you use an 8-inch skillet for this recipe: if the frittata is too thin, you'll end up with rubber; too thick, and you risk runny eggs.

1/2 pound morels

2 tablespoons unsalted butter

2 cloves garlic, thinly sliced

1 tablespoon chopped fresh summer savory

8 large fresh eggs, lightly beaten

Preheat the oven to 350°F.

To clean the morels, fill a large bowl with cool water. Dunk the mushrooms once or twice, then allow to dry on paper towels or a clean dishcloth for at least an hour. Stem the morels, then halve them lengthwise.

Heat the butter in an 8-inch ovenproof skillet or sauté pan over medium-high heat. Add the morels and sauté for 3 to 4 minutes to soften, then add the garlic and cook just until soft. Be careful not to let the garlic brown. Add the savory and eggs and stir gently.

Decrease the heat to medium and cook until the edges are just set and the bottom is browned, gently lifting the frittata with a metal spatula to check.

Transfer the pan to the oven and bake just until the center is set, 14 to 16 minutes. To check doneness, give the pan a little shake; if the center jiggles, give it a few more minutes. Remove from the pan and cut into wedges to serve.

Bruschetta with Fresh Ricotta and Pine Nut Salsa Verde

Make this with homemade ricotta and you will be rewarded with a starter that is rich, pretty, and piquant. It is perfect for entertaining, because you can prepare the crostini, ricotta mixture, and salsa verde ahead of time and put the bruschetta together when your guests arrive.

2 cups Fresh Ricotta (page 110)

$^1/_4$ cup extra-virgin olive oil, plus extra for brushing

1 baguette, sliced into 12 to 16 pieces (see page 10)

$^1/_3$ cup Salsa Verde (variation with pine nuts, page 219)

Before you begin, make sure all of your ingredients are at room temperature. Preheat your grill, if using. (You can also crisp the bread in a toaster.)

Combine the ricotta and oil in a metal bowl and whip with a whisk until fluffy. Alternatively, use a stand mixer with the paddle attachment and beat for 30 seconds to 1 minute, just to lighten the mixture and make sure the oil is incorporated.

Brush each slice of bread with a little olive oil, and then grill until lightly toasted and crisp, about 2 minutes per side. Alternatively, use a toaster to crisp the bread then brush with olive oil.

Spread the ricotta mixture over the crostini, about 2 tablespoons per slice. Dollop about 1 teaspoon of the salsa verde on each and serve.

Soft-Boiled Eggs with Anchovy Mayonnaise

Think of these as the most decadent, upscale version of a deviled egg you'll ever eat. But instead of rubbery eggs sprinkled with paprika, these soft-boiled beauties reveal moist, velvety yolks, accented by a luxe anchovy mayo. This is the recipe where you want your eggs to be as fresh as possible. Short of keeping your own chickens, go to your farmers' market and buy local. Don't get all freaked out if they have a bit of straw or dirt or, um, other debris on the shells. It means they're fresh, plus eggs have a natural antibiotic coating that protects them until you wash them. Inside, you'll find bright orange-yellow yolks and an incredible flavor that supermarket eggs just don't offer.

6 large fresh eggs

Kosher salt and freshly cracked pepper

Juice of 1/2 lemon

Anchovy Mayonnaise (recipe follows)

2 tablespoons chopped fresh parsley

Put the eggs in a pot and cover them with at least 1/2 inch water. Remove the eggs and bring the water to a soft boil. Prepare an ice-water bath.

When the water reaches a boil, gently lower the eggs into the water with a strainer or slotted spoon and cook for exactly 7 minutes. Immediately transfer the eggs to the ice bath. When cool, shell the eggs (shelling under water might make it easier if the shells are hard to remove). Halve the eggs and place on a platter.

Sprinkle with salt and pepper. Squeeze a few drops of lemon juice over each half. Place a dollop of the mayonnaise on each one, about 1 teaspoon. Sprinkle parsley over the eggs and serve.

ANCHOVY MAYONNAISE

1 fresh egg yolk

2 tablespoons water

1 teaspoon Dijon mustard

Juice of 1/2 lemon

5 anchovy fillets

1 1/2 cups canola oil

Kosher salt

Place the egg yolk, water, mustard, lemon juice, and anchovy fillets in a food processor. Pulse a few times to combine. With the motor running, add the oil in a slow, steady stream. Season to taste with salt.

Shigoku Oysters on the Half Shell with Accompaniments

Totten Virginicas, Stellar Bay Kusshis, and Shigoku oysters are my top three oysters. Shigokus are Pacific oysters raised in floating bags that rise and fall with the tide, creating a small, firm "tumbled" oyster in a scoop-shaped shell. They have an amazingly clean taste that hovers somewhere between saltwater and cucumber. Because their taste is so pure, I keep my garnishes straightforward. The Meyer Lemon Ice is a sweet, frozen version of a lemon squeeze, and the pickled beets are my idea of a mignonette. You can choose to prepare only one, but the array of all three, with oysters glistening on a bed of cracked ice, is one of the nicest ways I know to start an evening . . . or an afternoon.

You'll need crushed ice for serving the oysters. If you don't have a refrigerator that dispenses it, you can crush it in a food processor or blender. In the restaurants, we grind the ice ahead of time and put it in a colander over a bowl so some of the water drains out. Another trick is to line the bowl with paper towels to soak up any melting water while the oysters are being served.

24 fresh Shigoku oysters, top shells removed

MEYER LEMON ICE

Freshly cracked pepper

Juice of 3 Meyer lemons (about $^1/_2$ cup)

Extra-virgin olive oil, for drizzling

PICKLED YELLOW BEETS

1 cup champagne or other good-quality white vinegar

1 cup finely diced yellow beets

Minced chives, for sprinkling

GRANNY SMITH APPLE WITH HORSERADISH AND LEMON

$^1/_2$ lemon

1 Granny Smith apple, peeled and very finely diced

1-inch piece fresh horseradish

Place the oysters on a bed of crushed ice.

To make the lemon ice, add 2 twists of the pepper mill to the lemon juice and pour into a wide, flat dish that you can put in the freezer. A wide soup bowl or a glass or ceramic pie plate would work just fine. Freeze until hard, about 4 hours or overnight. Using the tines of a fork, scrape across the surface to create a fluffy, light lemon ice. Reserve in the freezer. (It's good to do this well in advance—a couple of days would be fine.)

To serve, top each oyster with about $^1/_2$ teaspoon of the lemon ice. Drizzle with a tiny bit of the finest olive oil.

To make the pickled beets, bring the vinegar JUST to a boil. Remove from the heat and add the beets. Pour into a heatproof container and place in the refrigerator to cool.

When ready to serve, top each oyster with $^1/_2$ teaspoon of the pickled beets and a little liquid. Sprinkle with the chives.

To make the apple and horseradish accompaniment, squeeze the lemon over the diced apple and set aside.

When ready to serve, spoon $^1/_2$ teaspoon of the mixture on top of each oyster. Grate a fine shower of fresh horseradish over the top of each.

Uni Spoons

Uni, or sea urchin roe, is at once delicate and incredibly rich. I like this preparation because the chive and radish offer a bit of bite and cut some of that richness, while the lemon and cucumber contribute a breezy freshness. Because the portions are small, make sure you cut the vegetables into a very fine, uniform dice. This would make a very elegant passed appetizer at a cocktail party. You can find fresh uni packaged in trays at Asian markets.

1 tray uni, about 4 ounces

$1/2$ cup small-diced cucumber

$1/2$ cup diced radish

Juice of 1 lemon

3 tablespoons extra-virgin olive oil

3 tablespoons minced chives

Gently separate the individual uni sacs and place on a decorative spoon (Chinese soup spoons make a fun presentation). Gently combine the cucumber, radish, lemon juice, olive oil, and chives and spoon a bit of the dressed vegetables over the top of each spoon. Serve immediately.

The Measure of a Cook: Soups

Looking through the recipes in this section, you might think these are some of the simplest preparations in the book. In a way, you would be right. These are also some of the most special, to my mind. A soup done right is a revelation and, in every way, the measure of a cook. Soup should be one of the most perfect and authentic expressions of an ingredient—its radiance, flavor, and essence encapsulated in the bowl.

When I eat out, often I won't order soup, even if it looks good on the menu, because I've been disappointed too many times. Soup should be made to order, like any other dish, and if it sits in a steam table for the day, it will suffer. Many well-meaning cooks don't take the time to cook their vegetables perfectly—just shy of being done—wrongly believing that it doesn't matter in a puréed soup.

I urge you to rethink your soup pot. Treat it to only the most precious and perfect of vegetables, grains, and meats, and cook them perfectly, just as you would if you were going to feature them in the middle of the plate. Whether the dish will be puréed, as in the Essence of Artichoke Soup, or will retain its textures and contrasts, as with the Corn and Chanterelle Soup, these delicate ingredients demand respect. It's important to add ingredients only when they should be added to ensure proper cooking time and retain their flavor, texture, and brilliant color.

Especially with puréed soups, proper cooling is just as important as proper cooking. If you will not be serving a soup immediately, take the time to chill the soup quickly in the refrigerator, set over an ice bath to hasten the process. I promise you will be rewarded with extraordinary flavor, texture, and color.

Essence of Artichoke Soup

I'm not the biggest fan of puréed soups, but this is the exception: the simplicity captures the vegetable's essence perfectly, and the texture is luscious and rich without even a bit of cream that might blunt the flavor. Take care to remove all of the green, fibrous leaves and bits when you prep the artichokes, and strain the soup through a fine-mesh sieve to ensure it's pure velvet. I like to retain the simplicity by garnishing with nothing more than a drizzle of excellent olive oil to highlight the color and flavor.

4 artichokes

2 tablespoons good-quality olive oil, plus more for drizzling

3 cloves garlic, thinly sliced

Kosher salt

4 cups water

To prepare the artichokes, first peel the fibrous outer covering from the stems, trimming only the very bottom and leaving as much stem intact as possible. (See step-by-step photos on pages 16 and 17.) Cut off the top of each artichoke with a very sharp chef's knife. Next, pull off all the tough outer leaves. Use kitchen shears to snip off the tops of the tender inner leaves. Quarter the artichoke and remove the choke from each quarter. Cut into 1-inch chunks.

Heat the olive oil in a stockpot or Dutch oven. Add the garlic and sauté just until soft. Add the artichokes, along with a pinch of salt, and stir to coat with the oil. Add the water and bring to a boil. Decrease the heat to a brisk simmer and cook until the artichokes are just tender—watch them carefully—10 to 12 minutes.

Purée the soup in batches in a blender or use a stick blender in the pot to form a smooth purée. Strain the soup through a chinois or fine-mesh sieve to remove any stray fibers.

Divide the soup among 4 bowls. Drizzle with a little good olive oil and serve.

SOUPS WITH ARTICHOKES

Artichokes might be my favorite vegetable. They're cool looking, number one, and the flavor is amazing—earthy and sweet, with a nearly bitter edge. I love them so much that I couldn't include just one artichoke soup in the book. The first recipe for artichoke soup is nothing more than the brilliant vegetable itself accented with a little garlic.

The Farro and Artichoke Soup is heartier—more peasant fare than elegant starter—but deeply satisfying with bright spring flavors. Once you've mastered prepping the artichokes you'll want to try them both.

Farro and Artichoke Soup

I don't generally use chicken stock in soups. I prefer the cleaner flavor that water brings to the soup, especially with such a fantastic vegetable as the artichoke. Farro is a chewy Italian grain somewhat like spelt, but with a firmer texture.

If you want to prepare the soup ahead of time, be sure to chill it immediately after cooking, transferring it to a shallow container so that it cools quickly. You'll need to adjust the water levels when you reheat the soup because the farro will absorb some of the water as it sits. For a nice variation, you could add some fava beans or peas.

1 lemon, halved

4 large artichokes

2 tablespoons good-quality olive oil, plus more for drizzling

3 cloves garlic, thinly sliced

1 cup farro

6 cups water

Kosher salt and freshly cracked pepper

2 tablespoons chopped fresh parsley

Fill a medium-size bowl with cool water. Squeeze the lemon juice into the bowl, then add the halves.

To prepare the artichokes, first peel the fibrous outer covering from the stems, trimming only the very bottom and leaving as much stem intact as possible. (See step-by-step photos on pages 16 and 17.) Cut off the top of each artichoke with a very sharp chef's knife. Next, pull off all the tough outer leaves. Use kitchen shears to snip off the tops of the tender inner leaves. Quarter the artichoke and remove the choke from each quarter. Slice thickly. Place the artichokes in the acidulated water and set aside.

Heat the olive oil in a stockpot or Dutch oven. Add the garlic and sauté until soft. Add the farro and stir to coat the grains with the oil. Add 2 cups of the water and bring to a boil. Decrease the heat to a simmer and cook until the water almost runs dry, about 10 minutes. The farro won't be completely cooked at this point, but this prevents it from overcooking as you finish the soup.

Add the artichokes and the remaining 4 cups water to the pot along with a good pinch of salt and a couple of grinds of cracked pepper. Simmer until the vegetables are just tender, 8 to 10 minutes. Add the parsley and stir. Serve in deep bowls, drizzled with olive oil.

Mediterranean Mussel and Chickpea Soup with Fennel and Lemon

My wife, Angela, loves mussels, especially the fat, tender Mediterranean mussels you get in summer and early fall. Consequently, we eat a lot of them—steamed, in salads, with pastas, you name it. Light enough for a summer dish, this terrific soup is also delicious in the winter months made with Prince Edward Island (P.E.I.) mussels instead.

2 tablespoons extra-virgin olive oil

3 cloves garlic, thinly sliced

Pinch of chile flakes

1 1/2 pounds fresh mussels, debearded and scrubbed

1 cup white wine

1 cup Basic Chickpeas (page 220)

1 small bulb fennel, tough outer leaves removed, sliced

Kosher salt and freshly ground pepper

Juice of 1 lemon

3 tablespoons chopped fresh parsley

Heat the olive oil in a large saucepan or Dutch oven over medium heat, and add the garlic and chile flakes. Before the garlic colors, add the mussels and white wine. Increase the heat to high, cover, and let the mussels steam for 3 to 4 minutes, or until they just open.

Discard any mussels that don't open and transfer the others to a baking dish with any cooking liquid that is in the pan. Set in the refrigerator until cool enough to handle. Once cool, remove the mussels from the shells, and discard the shells. (Note: You can keep the mussels in the fridge until ready to serve the soup, then proceed from this point.)

In a medium-size saucepan, combine the mussels, cooking liquid, chickpeas, and sliced fennel and heat through. The fennel should retain a bit of a bite. Season to taste with salt and pepper. Add the lemon juice and parsley. Serve immediately.

Clam Brodetto

This bright, sassy soup is full of big flavors—garlic, peppers, and lemon—that team up to accent the briny clams. The dish is then tamed, just a bit, with velvety Controne beans, one of my favorite Italian beans. Goat Horn peppers are red, slim peppers that you can find in Spanish and Italian markets, or in some upscale grocery stores. The preparation of this soup is fairly straightforward, and once you start cooking, the dish moves quickly. Have all of your ingredients prepared and ready before you begin.

3 tablespoons extra-virgin olive oil

1 Goat Horn pepper, chopped

1 teaspoon chile flakes

4 cloves garlic, sliced paper-thin

1 cup white wine

1 (14-ounce) can San Marzano tomatoes (see sidebar, page 216), passed through a food mill

2 pounds clams

1 cup Controne Beans (page 162)

Juice of 1 lemon

2 to 3 tablespoons chopped fresh parsley

Kosher salt and freshly ground pepper

Pour the olive oil into a deep sauté pan over medium-high heat and add the Goat Horn pepper, chile flakes, and garlic. Sauté until soft but not colored. Add the white wine and cook until the alcohol evaporates, 2 to 3 minutes.

Add the tomatoes and decrease the heat to a simmer. Cook for 8 to 10 minutes longer, until the mixture is thickened, then add the clams and beans and increase the heat. Cover immediately and cook over medium heat until the beans are heated through and the clams open, just a few minutes more. Discard any clams that don't open.

Just before serving, add the lemon juice and parsley. Season to taste with salt and pepper and serve.

Parmesan Brodo

Instead of cutting your knuckles trying to grate Parmesan close to the rind, keep your scraps in a resealable bag in your fridge. Once you've saved up about a pound's worth of odds and ends—which wouldn't take too long in my house—use them to make this rich, perfumed broth. Mushroom trimmings or pancetta pieces would also make nice additions, but avoid any vegetables that are too strongly flavored or they will overwhelm the flavor of the cheese.

1 pound Parmigiano-Reggiano rinds and ends

1 onion, peeled and halved

1 head garlic, halved crosswise

A few sprigs fresh parsley

1 gallon cold springwater

Combine all the ingredients in a large stockpot over high heat and bring to a boil. Decrease the heat to low and simmer for 1 hour to 1 hour and 15 minutes, until the broth is richly flavored and aromatic. Strain through a sieve lined with cheesecloth. Use immediately, or freeze in ice-cube trays, and then transfer to a large resealable bag. The broth will keep in the freezer for up to 2 months.

VARIATION: PROSCIUTTO BROTH

Use the same quantity (1 pound) prosciutto rinds, end, and bits. If you don't use as much prosciutto as I do and want to make the broth, ask your butcher for some scraps you can buy for cheap. Chill the broth and skim the fat before using or freezing.

Oxtail Soup with Farro and Root Vegetables

This soup uses a very simple technique that is time-consuming, to be sure, but requires very little attention and rewards you with loads of rich flavor. Consider this a Sunday afternoon on the back of the stove kind of dish. Although I use carrots, celery, celery root, and one of my favorite underutilized vegetables here—parsnips—you can use any variety of root vegetables that you have on hand or that look good at the market. Just be sure to use at least a few different kinds to lend real depth of flavor to the soup. I add the vegetables toward the end of cooking to keep the flavors bright and save them from turning to mush. Any leftovers will make Monday night dinner a snap, and the soup even improves if made in advance. Be sure to cool it properly in the fridge and taste for seasoning the next day. You may want to thin it with a little additional water if it's too thick upon reheating.

4 pounds oxtail

2 tablespoons extra-virgin olive oil

1 onion, diced

5 cloves garlic, sliced

1 cup farro

1 cup peeled and diced parsnip

1 cup diced carrot

1 cup peeled and diced celery root

1 cup diced celery

1/2 bunch Italian parsley, minced

Place the oxtail in a stockpot or Dutch oven over high heat and cover with 2 inches of water. Bring to a boil, then decrease the heat to low and simmer for 3 to 4 hours. Check the pot occasionally to skim off any foam and top off the water as necessary to keep the oxtail covered. Cook until the meat easily pulls away from the bone.

When the oxtail is ready, remove from the water with tongs and place on a sheet pan to cool. Strain the stock through a fine-mesh sieve or chinois and then skim the fat. You should have about 2 quarts of stock. If not, add water to make 2 quarts. Set aside. When the oxtail is cool enough to handle, remove the meat from the bones and discard the bones.

Heat the olive oil in a Dutch oven or stockpot over medium-high heat and add the onion and garlic. Sauté until the vegetables are soft but not colored. Add the farro and stir to coat in the oil. Add the stock and bring to a boil, then decrease the heat to low and simmer until the farro is almost tender, about 20 minutes.

When the farro is nearly tender to the bite, add the parsnip, carrot, celery root, celery, and oxtail meat. Simmer for about 20 minutes longer, or until the vegetables are tender. If making ahead, remove the soup from the heat at this point and put in the fridge to cool. If serving immediately, add the minced parsley and serve.

Farmers' Market Soup

I created this dish following a particularly inspirational visit to the farmers' market, one of those visits where every vegetable looks like something holy and you want to take home every variety laid out in front of you. Think of this soup as more of a philosophy than a recipe. Use the very best, freshest, tiniest baby spring vegetables you can find, either following the guidelines here or substituting whatever looks best in the market, then accent their sweetness with just a hint of mint, lemon verbena, or cicely. If you do use favas in the recipe, be sure to follow the directions here for removing their skins; using the traditional blanching method will result in overcooked beans.

The Cincinnati radish makes the soup a very pale, pretty pink that looks gorgeous served in shallow white bowls. Because this is such an easy soup to make, I also like to serve it in demitasse cups or small mugs as a walk-around first course for a relaxed spring get-together.

To remove the skins from the fava beans, place them in a bowl, then fill it with very hot tap water. Allow the beans to soak for 5 to 10 minutes. To check if they are ready, try to pinch the skin off a test bean. When the skins slip off readily, remove them from all the favas, drain, and set aside.

Trim, scrub, and thinly slice the carrots and radishes. Thinly slice the onion. Heat the olive oil in a large saucepan over medium-high heat. Add the onion, favas, and peas and sauté for 2 to 3 minutes, just enough for the onion to soften; the favas and peas should be bright. Season with salt. Add the carrots, radishes, water, and mint. Bring to a boil, then decrease the heat to low and simmer for no more than 4 minutes. Taste for seasoning, then serve in shallow bowls or small mugs or cups, drizzled with olive oil.

2 ounces shelled fava beans

2 ounces true baby carrots

2 ounces Cincinnati radishes

1 stalk spring onion, trimmed

1 tablespoon good-quality extra-virgin olive oil, plus more for drizzling

2 ounces shelled English peas

Kosher salt

3 cups springwater

2 tablespoons whole, small mint leaves or other fresh herb of your choice

English Pea Soup with Poached Duck Egg

The success of this deceptively simple soup depends on the use of perfectly fresh English peas and careful, brief cooking to preserve their delicate flavor. The unctuous duck egg gilds the lily, highlighting the vibrant sweetness and color of the peas. If you wish to make the soup in advance of serving, chill it quickly in an ice bath after straining and blending in the cream. When ready to serve, reheat the soup while you poach the eggs.

3 tablespoons unsalted butter

1 yellow onion, chopped

2 small cloves garlic, thinly sliced

Kosher salt and freshly cracked pepper

3 cups shelled English peas

4 cups sparkling water

1/4 cup heavy cream

2 tablespoons white vinegar

4 duck eggs

3 tablespoons minced chives

Extra-virgin olive oil, for drizzling

Heat the butter in a sauté pan over medium heat and add the onion, garlic, and a pinch of salt. Sauté until the vegetables are soft and clear. Add the peas and water, along with another pinch of salt to set the color of the peas. Increase the heat to high and bring to a boil. Decrease the heat to low and simmer just until the peas are tender, 4 to 5 minutes.

Purée the soup in batches in a blender, taking care not to fill the blender more than half full and covering the top with a kitchen towel to avoid splatters. When all the soup is puréed, strain through a chinois or fine-mesh sieve into a medium-size bowl. Stir in the cream and season to taste with salt and pepper. If not serving the soup immediately, place the bowl in an ice-water bath and chill until cold, then refrigerate.

Fill a medium-size saucepan with water to a depth of at least 3 inches and add the vinegar. Place the pan over low heat and bring to just below a simmer. Crack 1 egg and drain off most of the white, then tip the yolk into a ramekin or teacup. To avoid sticking, dip the ramekin or cup just below the surface of the water until the whites set, then slip the egg out of the cup and into the water. Repeat with the remaining 3 eggs. Poach the eggs to medium, 3 to 4 minutes, taking out the eggs in the reverse order they were placed in the pan. Retrieve each with a slotted spoon and place on paper towels to drain.

To serve, reheat the soup until hot. Divide the chives among 4 shallow bowls, sprinkling them on the bottom to provide a bed for the egg. Gently place a drained egg on top of the chives in each bowl. Carefully spoon or pour the soup around the egg. Gloss the egg with a bit of extra-virgin olive oil and sprinkle with kosher salt and cracked pepper. Serve immediately.

Kabocha and Porcini Soup

This hearty soup showcases the very best of fall—sweet kabocha squash and earthy porcini mushrooms—simmered together in a rich Parmesan broth. Using the Parmesan broth as a base adds indescribable depth, and as they simmer, the mushrooms perfume the broth and become tender and silky. I add just enough cream to give the soup body while allowing the flavors to shine through. If you can't find kabocha squash in your market, feel free to use other types of hard-skinned winter squash, such as butternut, or even sugar pumpkin.

1 pound porcini mushrooms

3 tablespoons unsalted butter

1^1/$_2$ cups peeled, diced kabocha squash

12 tiny cloves garlic, halved

Kosher salt and freshly ground pepper

8 sprigs thyme

4 cups Parmesan Brodo (page 47)

^{1}/$_4$ cup heavy cream

^{1}/$_4$ cup chopped fresh parsley

Wipe the mushrooms clean and trim the stems. Cut each mushroom into about 8 wedges.

Heat the butter in a large saucepan over medium-high heat. Add the mushrooms, squash, and garlic and cook until the garlic is tender, 2 to 3 minutes. Season to taste with salt and pepper.

Strip the leaves from the thyme sprigs and add the leaves to the pot along with the Parmesan broth. Bring to a simmer and cook for about 10 minutes, or until the squash is tender. Stir in the cream and parsley and serve.

Corn and Chanterelle Soup

When the late summer months bring you perfectly plump corn, buttery chanterelles, and Walla Walla onions so sweet you could eat them like apples, there isn't much to do but stay out of their way. This light but flavorful soup showcases each of the ingredients without overwhelming their delicacy. Because the corn and chanterelles offer such nice, contrasting textures, I prefer not to purée this soup.

2 plump ears fresh corn

2 tablespoons extra-virgin olive oil

1 Walla Walla onion, minced

2 fat cloves garlic, thinly sliced

$1/2$ pound chanterelles, wiped clean and quartered

Kosher salt and freshly ground pepper

1 teaspoon minced fresh summer savory

3 cups Parmesan Brodo (page 47)

Shuck the corn and remove all the silk. Stand 1 ear on end in a bowl to catch the kernels and the juice. Use a sharp knife to slice the kernels off the cob, then, using the dull edge of the knife, scrape down the sides of the cob, "milking" it into the bowl. Repeat with the second ear of corn. You should end up with about 2 cups of corn and juice.

Heat the olive oil in a deep pan over medium heat. Add the onion and garlic and sauté 4 to 5 minutes, until soft but not colored. Add the chanterelles and cook until soft, for 4 to 5 minutes longer, then season to taste with salt and pepper.

Increase the heat to high. Add the savory, corn and juice, and Parmesan broth. Bring to a boil, decrease the heat to low, and simmer the soup for 6 to 8 minutes, or until the corn is tender and the flavors have melded. Taste for seasoning and serve.

Heirloom Tomato Soup with Garlic Croutons

This isn't the kind of tomato soup that you eat with a grilled cheese sandwich, though it's about as easy to make. Because I like to concentrate the flavor of those amazing tomatoes, I keep the garnish here simple. I find the focaccia croutons add just enough contrast and crunch without taking away from the glory of the tomatoes. Use any combination of heirlooms that you like—from Black Russians to Green Zebras—just make sure they are juicy and ripe.

7 tablespoons extra-virgin olive oil

2 cloves garlic, halved, plus 1 clove garlic, slivered

1/4 day-old focaccia, cut into large cubes

3 pounds heirloom tomatoes, cored and cut into chunks

2 teaspoons Chianti vinegar

Kosher salt and freshly ground pepper

Preheat the oven to 350°F.

Heat 3 tablespoons of the olive oil in a small saucepan over medium heat and add the garlic halves. Allow the garlic to infuse the oil for 2 to 3 minutes, then toss the oil and garlic with the bread cubes. Spread on a baking sheet. Bake the cubes in the oven for 12 to 15 minutes, until crispy.

In a large bowl, toss the tomatoes with the remaining 4 tablespoons olive oil, the vinegar, and the slivered garlic, then season liberally with salt and pepper. Allow the tomatoes to marinate for at least 30 minutes at room temperature.

When ready to serve, purée the mixture in the blender with all the accumulated juices. Strain through a fine-mesh sieve. Divide among 4 shallow bowls and top each with a sprinkle of croutons.

Sorrel and Yogurt Soup

Wood sorrel, with shamrock-shaped leaves and a more mellow and elegant flavor than its cousin, grows wild across the United States. Common sorrel is easier to find, with more of a pronounced sour-lemony taste, and can be used in this recipe if foraging isn't one of your fortes. This is a refreshing soup, simple to make, with an elusive, unusual flavor due to the herb. Greek yogurt is thicker than other types of yogurt, but draining it still yields a denser base for the soup.

2 cups plain, full-fat Greek yogurt

3 cucumbers

Kosher salt and freshly ground pepper

2 tablespoons extra-virgin olive oil

2 ounces fresh wood sorrel, stems removed

Place the yogurt in a sieve and let drain over a bowl for 1 to 2 hours, until thickened. Peel the cucumbers, halve them lengthwise, then scrape out the seeds with the tip of a spoon. Slice, then toss with a large pinch of salt in a bowl. Allow to marinate while the yogurt drains.

Put the cucumbers, yogurt, and olive oil in a blender and purée. Add the sorrel leaves and blend until smooth. Strain through a fine-mesh sieve and season to taste with salt and pepper. Chill until cold. Taste again for seasoning after chilling, and then serve.

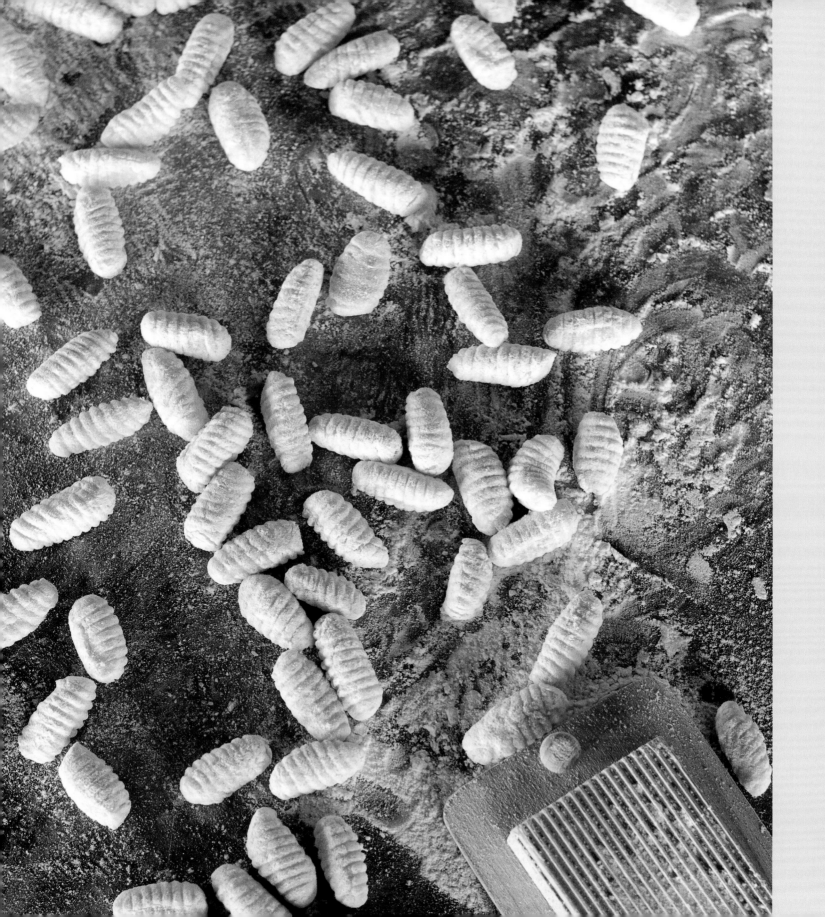

Starches to Grow On: Gnocchi, Polenta, Risotto, and Farrotto

On the face of things, gnocchi, polenta, risotto, and farrotto may seem like odd bedfellows. After all, gnocchi are mostly treated like pasta, while polenta stands in for potatoes or bread as a side. Risotto becomes a meal in itself, and is still offered as the sole "vegetarian" option in many restaurants. Farrotto is a similar dish crafted from farro, or emmer wheat. What they have in common is that all need to be prepared properly and delicately to fulfill their destiny on the plate. Each dish in this section is flavorful and restrained, offering a lighter dish more suited to modern palates.

Gnocchi, like soups, are an excellent yardstick by which to gauge a chef's skill. Whether crafted from ricotta or potatoes, gnocchi should have body—they're not doughnuts, after all—but should never be heavy or leaden and should cling to the sauce in which they are cloaked. Using baking potatoes that bake up light and fluffy gets you part of the way there and helps concentrate the flavor.

Polenta is one of my favorite sides to serve at the restaurants. There is such a sweet taste inherent in the corn, and it's easy to control the added fat while still creating a luxurious dish. A puddle of soft, steaming polenta is ideal for sopping up juices and creating textural contrast to seared and roasted meats. Sautéed or grilled polenta makes a sublime base for vegetables, from juicy heirloom tomatoes to silky mushrooms. Now that's a vegetarian option you'll be proud to serve.

Risotto and farrotto can be gummy and starchy in the wrong hands, or ethereal. It is a beautiful thing to make a perfect risotto, cooking it more quickly than is common so the rice retains a bit of bite and resisting the urge to stir until your arm falls off. Both limit the amount of starch the rice releases into the broth and result in a lighter dish.

Basic Potato Gnocchi

If you think you don't like potato gnocchi, you've probably been subjected to some heavy, leaden mistakes. The good news is that it's relatively easy to make your own, and following a few rules produces light, fluffy dumplings every time. First, it's essential to use russet (baking) potatoes, and to bake them with their skins on to ensure they don't soak up excess water from boiling and turn soggy. Peel the potatoes as soon as you can handle them, and mix the dough gently while the potatoes are still warm. If you're nervous about the consistency of your dough, simply blanch a test gnocchi in boiling water before forming and shaping them. If it falls apart in the water, you need to add a little more flour to the dough.

> 2 large russet potatoes, scrubbed
>
> Extra-virgin olive oil, for rubbing
>
> Kosher salt
>
> 2 large fresh egg yolks, at room temperature
>
> 1/2 cup "00" flour, plus more for dusting

Preheat the oven to 350°F. Place the potatoes on a baking sheet. Rub them with olive oil and sprinkle with salt, then place in the oven and bake for about 1 hour, or until tender. Transfer the potatoes to a rack and let rest until cool enough to handle.

Lay a sheet of parchment paper on a baking sheet. Put the potatoes through a ricer, letting them fall onto the parchment and discarding the skins as you go. Spread the potatoes out on the parchment and allow them to rest until warm, but not hot enough to cook the egg yolks. Gather up the parchment and dump the potatoes into a medium-size bowl.

Add the egg yolks to the potatoes and stir to combine. Sprinkle the flour over the top of the mixture and knead gently in the bowl until the egg and flour are distributed. Turn the dough out onto a floured board and continue to knead, adding extra flour as necessary, until the dough is no longer sticky.

Divide the dough into quarters. Roll each quarter into a log about 1/2 inch in diameter, then cut crosswise into 1-inch intervals. If your recipe calls for sautéing the gnocchi, you can leave them as little dumplings. If you want to create ridges to hold sauce, you can use either a gnocchi paddle or the tines of a fork. For the gnocchi paddle, roll each dumpling gently but firmly diagonally across the paddle, letting each dumpling fall onto a well-floured sheet pan as you finish. To use a fork, invert the fork so that the tines point down. Starting at the tines nearest the handle, roll the dumpling firmly but gently down the tines, creating a bit of a curve and ridges as you go, allowing the dumpling to fall off the ends of the tines and onto a well-floured baking sheet.

You can hold the gnocchi on a baking sheet, as long as they are not touching, for a few hours, but better yet, do as we do in the restaurants. We blanch them at this point, which enables you to hold the gnocchi for up to a day in the refrigerator.

To blanch, bring a pot of salted water to a boil. Cook the gnocchi, 15 to 20 at a time, just until they float to the surface, 1 to 2 minutes. Either add sauce and serve immediately, or place on an oiled baking sheet and cover with plastic wrap.

Gnocchi with Morels and Fried Duck Egg

If you are the kind of person who prefers a croque madame to a croque monsieur, the addition of the fried egg gilding the lily in a truly spectacular way, then this is the dish for you. Fresh pillows of gnocchi topped with earthy morels makes for a sublime dish all on its own. Top each dish with a fried duck egg, the soft yolk oozing under your fork . . . need I go on?

1/2 pound morel mushrooms

2 tablespoons unsalted butter, plus more for frying

2 cloves garlic, thinly sliced

1 recipe Basic Potato Gnocchi (page 60)

Kosher salt

4 duck eggs

Parmigiano-Reggiano, for shaving

Bring a large pot of salted water to a boil.

While the water comes to a boil, clean the morels. Fill a large bowl with cool water. Dunk the mushrooms, then allow to dry on paper towels or a clean dishcloth for at least 1 hour. Stem the morels, then halve lengthwise and set aside.

Heat the 2 tablespoons butter in a sauté pan over medium-high heat. Add the morels and sauté for 4 to 5 minutes, until silky. Add the garlic and sauté for a couple of minutes longer, until the garlic is tender but not brown.

When the water comes to a rolling boil, add the gnocchi. Cook just until the gnocchi surface, using a slotted spoon or spider to remove them, and add to the sauté pan. Gently toss the morels with the gnocchi, adding a tablespoon or two of pasta water if the mixture looks dry. Season to taste with salt and keep warm.

Heat a generous pat of butter in 1 large or 2 small sauté or frying pans. Fry the eggs gently over medium heat until the edges are crisp but the yolks are still runny. Sprinkle with salt.

Divide the gnocchi and mushrooms among 4 shallow bowls. Top each with a fried egg. Using a vegetable peeler, shave Parmigiano-Reggiano over each bowl and serve.

Ricotta Gnocchi with Beef Short Rib Ragu

Using fresh ricotta as the base for gnocchi creates pasta of incredible delicacy with a richness that stands up well to bold sauces such as the short rib ragu. Think of forming the gnocchi as a meditation, enjoying the process and the feel of the dough under your fingers. This is a great basic meat sauce that's a staple at Tavolàta. Using short ribs instead of ground chuck makes for better depth of flavor and richness. You can either grind the meat yourself if you have a grinder or an attachment for your mixer, or ask your butcher to grind it for you. This is a fairly thick ragu that goes especially well with ricotta gnocchi or freshly made pappardelle.

1 pound Fresh Ricotta (page 110), about 2 cups

2 fresh egg yolks

1 cup sifted "00" flour, plus more for dusting

Beef Short Rib Ragu (recipe follows)

One day before you plan to make the gnocchi, set the ricotta to drain in a sieve set over a bowl. Allow to sit overnight in the fridge. Discard the liquid that separates out and place the ricotta in a large bowl.

Add the egg yolks to the ricotta and mix well. Sprinkle about half of the flour over the top. Knead gently in the bowl until the flour is incorporated. Turn the dough out onto a floured board and knead in the remaining flour, a little bit at a time, until the dough is no longer sticky.

Using a bench scraper or sharp knife, cut the dough into quarters. Working with one quarter at a time, roll the dough into a rope about $3/4$ inch in diameter. Cut the rope crosswise at 1-inch intervals. Using the palm of your hand, take each piece and gently roll against the board to form a rough ball. Create a depression in each by flattening one edge slightly with your thumb. Repeat with the remaining dough.

Bring a pot of salted water to a slow boil. Make sure the water isn't boiling too vigorously or the gnocchi may disintegrate before they are cooked. Cook about 20 gnocchi at a time, dropping them into the water. Once the gnocchi have risen to the surface, cook for exactly 1 minute longer, then remove with a spider or slotted spoon. You can hold the gnocchi on an oiled sheet pan or in an oiled bowl while you cook the rest. Serve with the ragu.

BEEF SHORT RIB RAGU

2 tablespoons extra-virgin olive oil

1¹/₂ pounds ground boneless short ribs

1 cup finely diced carrots

1 cup finely diced onion

1 cup finely diced celery

4 cloves garlic, thinly sliced

1 cup white wine

2 (28-ounce) cans San Marzano tomatoes
(see sidebar, page 216)

2 fresh bay leaves

Heat the olive oil in a Dutch oven or a high-sided pan over high heat. When the oil is hot, add the ground meat. Brown the meat over medium-high heat for 8 to 10 minutes, stirring to break up any lumps.

Add the carrots, onion, celery, and garlic and cook until the vegetables are tender. Add the wine, stirring and scraping up any browned bits from the bottom of the pan.

Meanwhile, put the tomatoes and their liquid through a food mill or purée in a food processor and strain to remove the seeds. Add the purée to the pot and bring to a boil. Add the bay leaves.

Decrease the heat to low and simmer, uncovered, for 1¹/₂ to 2 hours, or until the meat is quite tender, stirring occasionally to prevent sticking. While the ragu is cooking, make sure that the liquid in the bottom doesn't run dry and cause scorching. If the liquid evaporates before the meat is tender, add a little water and stir. When the sauce is finished, it should be a thick sauce with good body. Remove the bay leaves and serve.

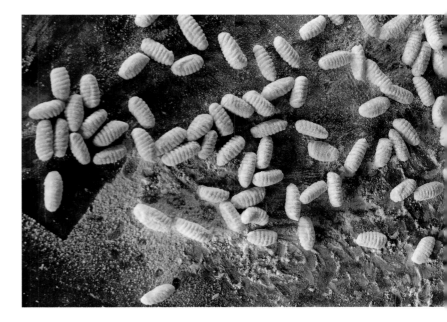

Polenta Master Recipes

I love polenta. I like that polenta is a starch where you can really control how much fat goes in, unlike mashed potatoes with all that butter and cream. I don't believe in spoiling that sweet corn taste by making it with chicken stock or adding all sorts of fancy extras. I don't even like to add pepper because I think it overpowers that delicate flavor. Polenta should be simple, creamy, and good. It makes the perfect pillow for dishes such as braised beef cheeks or for sautéed mushrooms for a nice first course. You can also pile it into a bowl and pass it at the table, just like mashed potatoes, only better. Alter the ratio a little and you can make hard polenta meant to be chilled, cut into shapes, then grilled or sautéed. Try it both ways to accompany different dishes.

SOFT POLENTA

SERVES 8

Adding the cornmeal to the water, and avoiding lumps, is the only challenging part of making good polenta. In the restaurants, we make it to order, and I vacillate between using fine and medium grinds, depending on the finished consistency I am looking for. The coarser polenta has more presence on the plate and such a deep corn flavor that I think it's a good place to start. Of course, fine or "instant" polenta has the advantage of being quicker to make. Traditionally, polenta is made using a wooden spoon, though I use a whisk. If you don't need or want this much polenta, you can halve the recipe with good results.

> $4^{1}/_{2}$ cups water
>
> 1 cup medium-grain polenta
>
> 1 packed cup finely grated Parmigiano-Reggiano
>
> Kosher salt

Put the water in a deep saucepan over high heat and bring to a boil. Slowly whisk in the polenta, adding it in a slow but steady stream and keeping the whisk moving. Decrease the heat to low and keep stirring, enough to avoid sticking. You'll notice when the grains swell and the polenta begins to thicken. Add the cheese and season with a little salt. You can hold the polenta for up to an hour in a metal bowl covered with plastic wrap. When ready to serve, you may need to whisk in up to $^{1}/_{4}$ cup additional hot water to restore the creamy texture.

FIRM POLENTA (FOR SAUTÉING OR GRILLING)

SERVES 8

When you pour out the polenta to chill, don't worry about making it pretty. Do what we do at the restaurants and use a cookie or biscuit cutter to create even shapes, or cut out wedges or squares—use your imagination. Grilled or sautéed polenta makes an excellent accompaniment to meat, game, or poultry. Try a couple of disks nestled next to a pork chop, roasted chicken, or guinea hen. Firm polenta should be crispy outside, soft and creamy inside, like a good French fry. In short, everything you could want.

3 cups water

1 cup medium-grain polenta

1 packed cup finely grated Parmigiano-Reggiano

Kosher salt

Extra-virgin olive oil, for sautéing or brushing

Put the water in a deep saucepan over high heat and bring to a boil. Slowly whisk in the polenta, adding it in a slow but steady stream and keeping the whisk moving. Decrease the heat to low and keep stirring, enough to avoid sticking. You'll notice when the grains swell and the polenta begins to thicken. Add the cheese and season with a little salt.

Pour out onto an ungreased plate or baking sheet. There's no need to make it perfect at this point; just make sure you spread it out fairly evenly about 1 inch thick. Put it in the fridge until it's cooled and set, at least a few hours or, better yet, overnight. The longer the polenta sits, the firmer it will become, making it hold together well when frying or grilling.

When the polenta is set, use a biscuit cutter, cookie cutter, or glass $1^1/_2$ to 2 inches in diameter to cut shapes from it. You should end up with 8 to 10 disks in all.

To fry, working in 2 sauté pans or 1 large one over high heat, heat enough olive oil to film the bottom of the pan. The pan should be very hot, nearly smoking, before you add the polenta, or it will stick. Add enough disks as will fit without crowding and brown the polenta for 2 to 3 minutes per side. As the polenta is browned, keep the disks on a wire rack set over a sheet pan. Reheat, if necessary, for about 6 minutes in a 300°F oven, before serving.

To grill, heat a grill or grill pan on high. Brush the polenta lightly with olive oil and grill, 2 to 3 minutes per side, or until grill marks appear and the polenta is heated through.

Sautéed Chicken Livers with Mushrooms and Onions on Soft Polenta

SERVES 4

This is my kind of comfort food—an accessible entrée to that old standby of liver and onions, yet fancy enough to be a company dish. Chicken livers have a deep, minerally flavor that I love, and they're economical to boot. Wild mushrooms accent the rich flavor with their own woodsy quality, while a silken puddle of polenta forms a savory pillow for the dish. Doesn't that sound better than meatloaf? This is a job for the biggest frying pan you have—the whole dish cooks in one pan.

4 cipollini onions

6 ounces wild mushrooms, wiped clean (about 3 cups)

Extra-virgin olive oil, for sautéing

1 pound chicken livers, cleaned of any fat and sinew

Kosher salt and freshly ground pepper

3 cloves garlic, sliced

1/2 cup white wine

3 tablespoons chopped fresh parsley

1/2 recipe Soft Polenta (page 66)

Peel the onions and cut them in half. Slice thinly. Cut off any tough stems from the mushrooms and halve them if they are large.

Film the bottom of your largest sauté pan with olive oil and heat over medium-high heat. Pat the livers dry with a paper towel and season generously with salt and pepper. When the oil is hot, add them to the pan and brown well on all sides. Transfer to a plate and drain the fat from the pan.

Return the pan to the heat and add a couple tablespoons of olive oil. Add the mushrooms, garlic, and onions and sauté for a minute or two, until soft. Return the chicken livers to the pan and add the wine, swirling to combine. Allow the mixture to cook down until the vegetables are tender and the livers are heated through and glazed with the wine, 2 to 3 minutes. At the last minute, add the parsley and toss to combine.

Puddle the polenta on 4 plates, making a depression in the center with the back of your spoon. Divide the chicken liver mixture among the plates, spooning it into the depression and drizzling with any juices.

Grilled Polenta with Heirloom Tomatoes and Pounded Anchovy Sauce

Seattle summers are our best-kept secret—with long, lovely days just hot enough to make you want to stay out of the kitchen and linger outside. The perfect appetizer for a patio barbecue, grilled polenta is easy, crisp, and luscious, and is played to its best advantage when topped with juicy heirloom tomatoes brightened with garlic and anchovy. If you like, substitute basil or another favorite tender herb for the mint. This would also be nice served with a handful of baby greens on the plate.

6 anchovy fillets, with a splash of their oil

1/2 clove garlic

Kosher salt and freshly ground pepper

10 fresh mint leaves

Juice of 1 lemon

1/4 cup extra-virgin olive oil

1 to 1 1/2 pounds sweet, ripe heirloom tomatoes (roughly 1 tomato per person)

1/2 recipe Firm Polenta (page 67), chilled

Preheat the grill on high.

With a mortar and pestle, pound together the anchovies, splash of anchovy oil, garlic, pinch of salt, and mint into a paste. Add the lemon juice and continue to blend with the pestle, then dribble in the olive oil. Stir to combine.

Core the tomatoes, cut into thin wedges, and divide among 8 plates. Sprinkle with salt and pepper.

Grill the polenta for 2 to 3 minutes per side, or until the wedges show grill marks and are heated through. Place 1 polenta wedge next to the tomatoes on each plate and drizzle with the anchovy sauce. Serve while the polenta is hot.

Sautéed Polenta with Hedgehog Mushrooms and Aged Provolone

Hedgehog mushrooms are close relatives to chanterelles, with a similar flavor profile but a little bigger. They are abundant beginning in mid-winter; if you can find them in the market, grab them up. Their richness makes them a fantastic match for aged provolone and crispy polenta. This dish makes a great side, but it is also substantial enough to make vegetarian guests very, very happy. If you like, you can grill the polenta instead of sautéing it.

3/4 pound hedgehog mushrooms

1/2 recipe Firm Polenta (page 67), chilled

3 tablespoons unsalted butter

1 shallot, minced

2 tablespoons chopped fresh parsley

3 tablespoons extra-virgin olive oil

1/4 pound aged provolone, for shaving

Wipe the mushrooms clean, trim off any woody stems, and slice lengthwise into quarters.

Using a cookie cutter or a sharp knife, cut the polenta into 6 desired shapes.

Heat the butter in a large sauté pan over high heat and add the shallot. Sauté for 2 to 3 minutes, until softened. Add the mushrooms and cook, stirring occasionally, until the mushrooms soften and give off their liquid, 3 to 4 minutes. Continue cooking until the mushrooms begin to color. Add the parsley, toss, and keep warm.

Film the bottom of a separate sauté pan with olive oil and heat over medium-high heat. Add the polenta slices and cook, without moving, until the bottoms are light brown and a crust has formed, about 2 minutes. Using a metal spatula, turn the polenta slices and cook 2 minutes more, or until the polenta is heated through.

Divide the polenta among 6 plates and top with the mushrooms. Using a vegetable peeler, shave the aged provolone over each dish.

Spring Garlic Risotto

Otherwise known as green garlic and garlic shoots, spring garlic captures the essence of garlic without any harshness or bite. Unlike mature garlic, spring garlic should be featured in recipes that won't overwhelm the delicate flavor, such as this risotto. Make sure you wash the spring garlic thoroughly to remove any sand.

3^1/$_2$ cups chicken stock

2 tablespoons unsalted butter

8 stalks spring garlic, thinly sliced (about 1^1/$_2$ cups)

1 cup carnaroli rice

^{1}/$_2$ cup white wine

Kosher salt

1 cup grated Parmigiano-Reggiano

Extra-virgin olive oil, for drizzling

Heat the stock in a saucepan and keep warm on the stove.

Heat the butter in a large sauté pan over medium heat. Add the garlic and sauté until soft but not colored, 2 to 3 minutes. Add the rice and stir to coat. Add the wine and cook, stirring, until the wine is absorbed by the rice. Add a pinch of salt.

Add 1 cup of the chicken stock. Cook, stirring occasionally, until the stock is absorbed, 5 to 6 minutes. Add another cup of stock, stirring, until absorbed. Add the remaining 1 cup stock in stages—not all of the stock may be necessary. When finished, the rice should be toothsome but not crunchy. If necessary, continue to add liquid to achieve the desired consistency. When that liquid has been absorbed, add the grated cheese and stir gently. Season to taste with salt.

Divide among 4 plates. Drizzle with olive oil and serve.

A TRIO OF SPRING RISOTTOS

• Spring Garlic Risotto
• Ramp Risotto with Shaved Porcini
• Artichoke Risotto

Many consider risotto a winter dish. I want to change that, and hope to tempt you with this collection of lovely dishes featuring some of the most delicate and glorious tastes of spring. Light enough to share the table with other dishes, these creamy beauties are bright in flavor and feature a range of spring time hues.

Ramp Risotto with Shaved Porcini

This risotto is a special springtime treat, not only because of the delicate flavor of the ramps but also because the porcini is allowed to really be the star. I treat it like a fine truffle, shaving it with a mandoline in a shower over each bowl. The heat of the risotto softens the mushrooms ever so slightly, and the shavings add texture and a wonderful fragrance

3 cups chicken stock

2 tablespoons unsalted butter

$1/2$ pound of ramps, stalks thinly sliced and leaves chopped (about $1^1/2$ cups)

1 cup carnaroli rice

$1/2$ cup white wine

Kosher salt

1 cup grated Parmigiano-Reggiano

Extra-virgin olive oil, for drizzling

$1/4$ pound small, extra-firm fresh porcini, wiped clean

Heat the stock in a saucepan and keep warm on the stove.

Heat the butter in a large sauté pan over medium heat. Add the ramps and sauté until soft but not colored, 2 to 3 minutes. Add the rice and stir to coat. Add the wine and cook, stirring, until the wine is absorbed by the rice. Add a pinch of salt.

Add 1 cup of the chicken stock. Cook, stirring occasionally, until the stock is absorbed, 5 to 6 minutes. Add another cup of stock, stirring, until absorbed. Add the remaining 1 cup stock in stages—not all of the stock may be necessary. When finished, the rice should be toothsome but not crunchy. If necessary, continue to add liquid to achieve the desired consistency. When that liquid has been absorbed, add the cheese and stir gently. Season with salt to taste.

Divide among 4 plates and shave the porcini over each using a mandoline. Drizzle with olive oil and serve.

Artichoke Risotto

I've met a lot of people who are so intimidated by the process it takes to extract the luscious heart from a large thistle that they never go any further with the artichoke than steaming it and melting some butter. There's nothing wrong with that approach—it's good eating, for sure—but it does keep you from enjoying a host of dishes that allow this regal vegetable to play a more suave, starring role.

The single most common mistake people make when they prep an artichoke is to use a dull knife. Not only home cooks make that mistake, either. I've seen professionals prep artichokes so they look like they went through the dryer. Take a steel to your knife and follow the directions carefully, and prepping the hearts should be a breeze, giving you the star ingredient for a lovely spring risotto.

This risotto takes a bit more liquid than some others in the book because the artichokes absorb some as they cook. Make sure the butter you add to finish the dish is cold, so it incorporates and adds richness and body.

1 lemon

2 globe artichokes, trimmed and sliced

4 cups chicken stock

2 tablespoons unsalted butter, plus 2 tablespoons, chilled

1 small red onion, minced

1 cup carnaroli rice

$^1/_2$ cup white wine

1 cup grated Parmigiano-Reggiano

Kosher salt

Extra-virgin olive oil, for drizzling

Fill a medium bowl with cool water. Cut the lemon in half. Squeeze the juice into the bowl, then add the halves. This acidulated water will keep your artichokes from turning brown before cooking.

To prepare the artichokes, first peel the fibrous outer covering from the stems, trimming only the very bottom and leaving as much stem intact as possible. (See step-by-step photos on pages 16 and 17.) Cut off the top of each artichoke with a very sharp chef's knife. Next, pull off all the tough outer leaves. Use kitchen shears to snip off the tops of the tender inner leaves. Quarter the artichoke and remove the choke from each quarter. Slice about $^1/_4$ inch thick. Place the artichokes in the acidulated water and reserve.

Heat the stock in a saucepan and keep warm on the stove.

Heat 2 tablespoons of the butter in a large sauté pan over medium heat. Add the onion and sauté until soft but not colored, 2 to 3 minutes. Add the rice and stir to coat. Add the wine and cook, stirring, until the wine is absorbed by the rice.

Add 1 cup of the stock. Cook, stirring occasionally, until the stock is absorbed, 5 to 6 minutes. Add the sliced artichokes and stir to incorporate. Add another cup of stock, stirring, until absorbed. Add the remaining $^1/_2$ cup stock. When finished, the rice should be toothsome but not crunchy. If necessary, continue to add liquid to achieve the desired consistency. When that liquid has been absorbed, add the cheese and stir gently. Finally, add the remaining 2 tablespoons chilled butter and gently fold the butter in until the risotto is shiny and creamy. Season with salt to taste.

Divide among 4 plates. Drizzle with olive oil and serve.

Clam Risotto with Lemon

This is a wonderful winter dish—fresh and simple with nothing to get between you and pure clam flavor. Steaming the clams first in a little white wine, then using that liquid in place of broth, infuses the rice with a briny essence that totally sings. Because of the star ingredient, you shouldn't need to use much salt in the dish, and cheese here would be a no-no. A little butter at the end provides the perfect touch of richness, while a bit of lemon zest accents the clams perfectly.

4 tablespoons extra-virgin olive oil, plus more for drizzling

6 cloves garlic, thinly sliced

4 pounds Manila clams

1 cup white wine

1 small red onion, minced

1 cup carnaroli rice

4 tablespoons unsalted butter

1 lemon (preferably organic)

In a high-sided sauté pan or Dutch oven over medium-high heat, heat 2 tablespoons of the olive oil. Add 3 cloves of the garlic and sauté for a minute or two, until soft. Add the clams and wine, cover and steam just until the clams open, 2 to 3 minutes.

Discard any clams that fail to open. Strain and reserve the liquid. You should have about 4 cups liquid; if you don't, add water to make 4 cups. Place in a saucepan and set over low heat until hot. Put the clams in a heatproof container and place in the refrigerator until cool enough to handle. For easy eating, shuck the clams when cool. Discard the shells and reserve the meat. For a fancier presentation, leave the clams as is.

In a large sauté pan over medium heat, heat the remaining 2 tablespoons olive oil. Sauté the remaining 3 cloves garlic and the onion until soft but not browned, 2 to 3 minutes. Add the rice and stir to coat. Add the reserved liquid, 1 cup at a time, stirring until the liquid is absorbed, 5 to 6 minutes, before the next addition. When finished, the rice should be toothsome but not crunchy. If necessary, continue to add liquid to achieve the desired consistency. When the rice is just al dente, remove the pan from the heat and fold in the clams and butter until the risotto is glossy.

Divide the risotto among 4 warm plates. Drizzle each plate with olive oil. Grate lemon zest over the top of each plate and serve.

Butternut Squash Risotto with Hazelnut Oil

Roasting the squash before incorporating it into the rice concentrates the flavor and adds great depth to this vibrant fall risotto. I use butternut here, but any firm-fleshed fall squash or pumpkin would work; kabocha would make an especially nice substitute. Cold-pressed hazelnut oil has a distinctive, nutty flavor, less pungent than some other nut oils, such as walnut. You can find some good brands from France, and one or two nice local oils that hail from the nut orchards of the Northwest. Although it's expensive, it's a great oil to use on salads and with certain desserts.

1 medium butternut squash, halved lengthwise

7 tablespoons unsalted butter

2 to 3 sprigs thyme

2 cloves garlic, smashed with the flat side of a chef's knife

Extra-virgin olive oil, for drizzling

Kosher salt

4 cups chicken stock

$^1/_2$ onion, minced

1 cup carnaroli rice

1 cup white wine

1 cup loosely packed grated Parmigiano-Reggiano

Hazelnut oil, for drizzling

Preheat the oven to 400°F.

Place each squash half on a square of aluminum foil and dot each with 1 tablespoon of the butter. Chop a few springs of thyme in half and add to the cavities along with 1 garlic clove each. Drizzle with olive oil and sprinkle with salt. Wrap each half in the foil and place on a baking sheet. Roast in the oven until tender, 1 hour to 1 hour and 15 minutes. Remove from the oven, remove from the foil, and set the squash aside to cool.

When the squash is cool enough to handle, scoop out the flesh and put through a sieve to catch any fibers. You should end up with about $1^1/_2$ cups of smooth purée.

Heat the stock in a saucepan and keep warm on the stove.

In a large sauté pan over medium heat, heat 2 tablespoons of the butter. Add the onion and sauté until soft but not colored, 2 to 3 minutes. Add the rice and stir to coat. Add the wine and cook, stirring, until the wine is absorbed by the rice, 5 to 6 minutes. Add a pinch of salt.

Add 1 cup of the stock. Cook, stirring occasionally, until the stock is absorbed. Add another cup of stock, stirring, until absorbed, 5 to 6 minutes. Add the squash purée and stir to incorporate, then add another cup of liquid. When this stock is absorbed, taste the rice. It should still have some chew but be tender to the bite. If necessary, add the remaining 1 cup stock in stages until the rice reaches the desired consistency. Remove the pan from the heat and add the cheese and remaining 3 tablespoons butter. Stir gently and season to taste with salt.

Divide among 4 plates. Drizzle with hazelnut oil and serve.

Farrotto with English Peas and Morels

Farrotto is a risotto-style dish made with farro instead of rice, but the similarity stops there. Farrotto has a greater depth and nuttiness than regular risotto—not better or worse, just different. It also produces a more textured final dish. It's out of this world paired with spring's first earthy morels and peas, which add sweetness and dots of color.

For tips on cleaning morels, see page 34. Farro is emmer wheat, often erroneously called "spelt" in English; you can find true farro in fancy grocery stores or specialty Italian markets.

2³/₄ cups chicken stock

1¹/₂ cups shelled English peas

6 tablespoons unsalted butter

3 cloves garlic, thinly sliced

1 small onion, minced

1 cup farro

¹/₂ cup white wine

2 tablespoons extra-virgin olive oil

¹/₂ pound morels, cleaned, stemmed, and quartered lengthwise

Kosher salt and freshly ground pepper

1 cup grated Parmigiano-Reggiano

3 tablespoons chopped fresh parsley

Place the stock in a saucepan and set over low heat to keep hot.

In a large saucepan or pot over high heat, bring salted water to a boil. Prepare an ice bath in a strainer set into a large bowl. Add the peas to the boiling water and blanch for 2 minutes. Immediately transfer to the ice bath. When cool, drain and reserve.

In a high-sided sauté pan or Dutch oven over medium-high heat, heat 2 tablespoons of the butter. Add the garlic and onion and sauté for 2 to 3 minutes. Add the farro and stir to coat. Add the wine and cook, stirring occasionally, until the wine is absorbed, 5 to 6 minutes.

Add 1 cup of the stock. Cook until the liquid is almost completely absorbed, 6 to 7 minutes, stirring occasionally.

While the farrotto is cooking, heat the olive oil in a medium sauté pan over medium-high heat. Add the morels and sauté until tender, 4 to 5 minutes. Remove from the heat and reserve.

Add 1 more cup stock to the farrotto. Continue cooking until the liquid is almost completely absorbed, 6 to 7 minutes, stirring occasionally. Add ¹/₂ cup more stock. When the liquid is nearly absorbed, taste the farrotto. It should be nearly tender with some resilience. Add the peas and the morel mixture with an additional ¹/₄ cup stock. Stir, and season to taste with salt and pepper. Remove from the heat and fold in the cheese and the remaining 4 tablespoons butter. Sprinkle with parsley and serve.

Duck Leg Farrotto with Pearl Onions and Bloomsdale Spinach

Duck breasts are delicious—that crackling skin and fat, the tender, ruby-hued meat. Duck legs do even more for me; the meat is darker, richer, and full of incredible flavor. If you plan on making a duck breast for dinner, buy a whole duck and roast the legs just so you can make this dish. Alternatively, I suppose you could buy a roasted duck from a Chinese barbecue and pick the meat.

Bloomsdale is a lovely, crinkly variety of spinach that is full-bodied and flavorful. If you can't find Bloomsdale, any heirloom or organic spinach will do. Make sure you wash the leaves well, dunking a few times to remove all the sand and grit.

4 cups Parmesan Brodo (page 47)

2 roasted duck legs

6 tablespoons unsalted butter

3 cloves garlic, thinly sliced

1 small onion, minced

1 cup farro

$1/2$ cup white wine

2 tablespoons extra-virgin olive oil

1 (8-ounce) bag pearl onions, peeled and halved lengthwise

1 bunch Bloomsdale spinach, washed well

Kosher salt and freshly ground pepper

1 cup grated Parmigiano-Reggiano

Place the broth in a saucepan and set over low heat to keep hot.

Pick the meat off the duck legs and discard the bones. You should end up with about $1^1/_2$ cups of loosely packed meat.

In a high-sided sauté pan or Dutch oven over medium-high heat, heat 2 tablespoons of the butter. Add the garlic and minced onion and sauté for 2 to 3 minutes, or until soft. Add the farro and stir to coat in the butter, then add the wine and cook, stirring occasionally, until the wine is absorbed, 5 to 6 minutes.

Add 1 cup of the broth. Cook until the liquid is almost completely absorbed, 6 to 7 minutes, stirring occasionally.

While the farrotto is cooking, heat the olive oil in a sauté pan over high heat. Add the pearl onions and sauté until well browned in spots and tender, 4 to 5 minutes. Remove from the heat and reserve.

Add 1 more cup broth to the farrotto and continue cooking until the liquid is almost completely absorbed, 6 to 7 minutes, stirring occasionally. Add another $1^1/_2$ to 2 cups broth in $1/_2$-cup additions. After each addition, continue tasting the farrotto for doneness. It should be nearly tender with some resilience. Add the duck meat, spinach, and pearl onions. Cook until the spinach is completely wilted, then season to taste with salt and pepper.

Remove from the heat and fold in the cheese and the remaining 4 tablespoons butter. The farrotto should be creamy and glossy. Serve.

Wheat's Highest Calling: Pasta

We're down in the "belly of the beast," the basement kitchen at Tavolàta, where every day we make fifty to sixty pounds of fresh pasta for the restaurants, plus two full sheet pans of agnolotti, fifteen pounds of potato gnocchi, a hundred semolina dumplings. . . . At one end of the kitchen sits an industrial giant, an Italian immigrant that makes pasta the old-fashioned way, an auger gently working the dough as water is dribbled in drop by drop, which is imperative if the water is going to be absorbed slowly. When the dough is cohesive enough to form a dough, the auger slams it against the die. The dough slides through the gleaming brass dies like Play-Doh through a garlic press; the smooth ropes, coiled and cut, nestle in beds of semolina.

Pasta was the first dish I cooked where the chef explained to me the rationale behind the proportions. A little water kept the consistency and bite. Good flour provided the flavor—the flavor!—not just body. Not too many egg yolks; you want the richness, but don't want to mask the delicate taste of the wheat. I've retained a strong reverence for pasta, for how it is made and for saucing it correctly. You should be able to taste the pasta with the sauce as an accent, a vehicle for the pasta—not the other way around.

Forget fried chicken or meatloaf and mashed potatoes—pasta is the very definition of comfort food. You make it with your bare hands, after all; you knead it, not aggressively but gently, then roll it and cut it, all the while keeping in mind who you are making it for. You cook it gently, too—not in rapidly boiling water, but in salted water kissed by bubbles. There is something heartwarming and deep about making a food this humble, and doing it lovingly and with care.

There are some company dishes in this section. There is a big wow factor in encasing a whole duck egg yolk in pasta, only to have it broken by the diner's fork. Fava beans and ricotta agnolotti are a bit of work, yes, but the richness played against sautéed snails is nothing short of spectacular. But don't overlook the simple beauty of Linguine with Shrimp, a dish where the flavor of the pasta enhances the sweetness of the seafood, a quick shrimp stock adding surprising depth to a bright tomato sauce. Or maybe it's sea urchin forming a creamy emulsion and coating strands of spaghetti, accented only with a bit of chile and garlic. Fresh, silky tagliarini cradles perfectly poached oysters, prosecco, and cream.

You don't need an Italian machine with brass dies to make beautiful pasta. A food processor makes gorgeous dough, and kids love sheeting dough on a twenty-dollar, hand-cranked machine. Add a fairly inexpensive attachment to your stand mixer and you can turn out amazing extruded pastas, too, in your own kitchen. I hope the recipes in this section allow you to discover for yourself the glory of a humble bowl of pasta, made with love and care.

Pasta Master Recipes

Fresh pasta dough is easy to make yourself, and the rewards in terms of texture and taste are phenomenal. Once you've mastered these two recipes, you'll find yourself having homemade pasta often. The lightest pasta is made with "00" flour, though you can substitute all-purpose flour if you can't find it. I like to use the egg dough with lighter pastas, filled pastas, or delicate sauces, such as the fava-ricotta agnolotti. The semolina dough holds up to "bigger" sauces, with the semolina creating a more distinct, stronger flavor even without the egg.

EGG PASTA

4 cups "00" flour

8 large fresh egg yolks, at room temperature

2 tablespoons extra-virgin olive oil

$^3/_4$ to 1 cup water

Place the flour, egg yolks, and olive oil in a food processor and process to combine. Using the feed tube, slowly add the water, pulsing between additions. The dough will just start to come together and shouldn't form a ball. Remove the dough from the food processor and place on a floured board. Knead by hand until the dough is soft and satiny, about 2 minutes. Wrap the dough tightly in plastic wrap and allow to sit on the counter for at least 30 minutes. This gives the gluten a chance to relax before you roll the pasta (see right).

SEMOLINA PASTA

4 cups semolina flour

$1^1/_2$ cups water

Follow the instructions for Egg Pasta, removing the dough to a semolina-dusted board after adding the water. This dough is a bit harder to work with and will require a good 3 to 4 minutes of vigorous kneading to develop the gluten. Wrap tightly in plastic wrap and allow to rest as with the Egg Pasta.

To roll either type of pasta, first cut each dough in half and keep the other half wrapped in plastic while you work with the first half. Dust the dough liberally with flour before and between rolling. Begin on the highest setting for your roller, working your way down to #1 thickness for pappardelle.

As you roll on the final setting, dust and fold the dough over in foot-long segments. With a sharp knife, cut horizontally at 1-inch intervals. Put on a baking sheet and toss with semolina. You can leave the cut pasta on a baking sheet or on a wire rack for a few hours before cooking. Pasta that has been allowed to sit tends to stick together while cooking, so give the pasta a vigorous stir when you first put it in boiling water.

Braised Rabbit Paws with Radiatore

Americans don't eat as much rabbit as they should, and it's a shame. Rabbit meat is light and clean tasting, and the legs make a delicate braise without the heaviness of beef or pork. I like to pair this braise with radiatore, a squat, square pasta with ruffles that really catch and hold the meat and the sauce.

Ask your butcher to piece out the rabbit for you, then save the more delicate loin—the strips that run along the back—for a quick-cooking preparation, such as the salad on page 112. As with chickens, rabbits are sold as both fryers and roasters, the fryers being smaller and younger with more tender flesh. That's the bunny you want.

2 tablespoons extra-virgin olive oil, plus more for drizzling

4 rabbit legs

Kosher salt and freshly cracked pepper

2 carrots, peeled and coarsely chopped

1 onion, peeled and coarsely chopped

6 cloves garlic, smashed with the flat side of a chef's knife

2 cups white wine

2 cups chicken stock

3 fresh bay leaves

5 sprigs fresh thyme

$^3/_4$ pound radiatore

8 small sage leaves

Freshly grated Parmigiano-Reggiano, for serving

Preheat the oven to 350°F.

Heat the olive oil in a Dutch oven or other large, heavy ovenproof pot over high heat. Season the rabbit legs with the salt and pepper and place in the Dutch oven. Brown well on both sides, 3 to 4 minutes each side, and then transfer to a plate. Pour off any excess oil but leave any fond, or the browned bits, stuck to the bottom.

Put the carrots, onion, and garlic in the same pot and sauté over high heat, scraping the bottom. Cook the vegetables until they soften and get a little color, 2 to 3 minutes. Return the rabbit legs to the pot, along with any accumulated liquid from the plate. Add the wine and stock. The liquid should come about three-quarters of the way up the sides of the legs. Add the bay leaves and thyme and bring to a boil. Cover the Dutch oven with a tight-fitting lid or foil and place in the oven. Braise for $1^1/_2$ to 2 hours, or until the rabbit pieces are tender.

Transfer the rabbit pieces to a plate to cool and remove and discard the herbs. Put the liquid and vegetables through a food mill fitted with the medium disk. Put this sauce in a large saucepan and keep warm over low heat.

When cool enough to handle, remove the meat from the bones. Discard the bones and chop the meat finely with a chef's knife. Add the meat to the sauce and stir to combine. Heat on medium-low to blend the flavors and add body.

Just before serving, bring a pot of salted water to a boil. Add the radiatore and cook according to the package directions until al dente. While the pasta cooks, slice the sage leaves into thin strips. Drain the pasta and add to the sauce in the saucepan, along with the sage. Stir to combine.

Divide the pasta among 4 bowls, drizzling each with a little extra-virgin olive oil. Pass the cheese at the table.

Linguine with Shrimp

The simple name of this dish doesn't tell you how **phenomenal it truly is, especially if you wait until you get your hands on large, just-out-of-the-water shrimp with the shell on. Use the shells to make a quick shrimp stock that acts as a building block of flavor to my basic tomato sauce, transforming the pasta into something special. Freeze the leftover shrimp stock in small yogurt containers and use to make linguine with shrimp again, or use with fish or seafood stews or risotto.**

Kosher salt and freshly ground pepper

2 cups Basic Tomato Sauce (page 216)

1 cup Shrimp Stock (recipe follows)

3/4 pound linguine

1 1/2 pounds fresh shell-on shrimp, 10–12 or 12–16 count

2 tablespoons chopped fresh Italian parsley

Extra-virgin olive oil, for drizzling

Set a pot of water to boil over high heat. Add a small handful of salt.

In a deep sauté pan set over medium heat, combine the tomato sauce and Shrimp Stock and bring to a simmer. Continue to cook for 10 to 15 minutes—you're not looking to reduce the sauce, just mingle the flavors.

When the water reaches a boil, add the pasta and cook for 1 minute less than the package directions say or until slightly firmer than al dente. While the pasta cooks, add the shrimp to the sauce and simmer just until pink, 2 to 3 minutes.

When the pasta is ready, drain and add to the shrimp and sauce, along with the parsley. Season to taste with salt and pepper. Divide among 4 plates, distributing the shrimp evenly among the plates. Drizzle each with extra-virgin olive oil and serve.

SHRIMP STOCK

2 tablespoons extra-virgin olive oil

Shells from 1 pound (or more) shrimp

3 cloves garlic

1 small onion, peeled and quartered

3 ribs celery, cleaned and chopped

1/2 cup white wine

In a medium saucepan, heat the olive oil and sauté the shells and garlic for 2 to 3 minutes, or until the shells turn pink. Add the onion, celery, and wine and bring to a boil. Add water to cover, bring to a boil, then simmer for 20 to 30 minutes to get the flavor out of the shells. Strain, pressing on the shells.

Cavatelli with Cuttlefish, Spring Onion, and Lemon

This is a great dish to bridge the end of winter with the beginning of spring. The bite of the garlic and chile is balanced by the mild flavor of spring's first onions. Long, oblong, and pretty, spring onions are the first indication to me that fresh garbanzos and nettles are on the way, signaling the end of butternut squash and other winter vegetables. If you can't find cuttlefish, you may use fresh calamari instead, though the cavatelli is a nice balance for the size and texture of the cuttlefish.

Kosher salt and freshly ground pepper

8 ounces cavatelli

2 bulbs spring onion, thinly sliced

3 cloves garlic, thinly sliced

1 teaspoon chile flakes

1/4 cup extra-virgin olive oil, plus more for drizzling

1 pound cuttlefish, washed, sliced into 1-inch slices, then sliced on the diagonal into thin strips

1 tablespoon chopped fresh parsley

Zest of 1/2 Meyer lemon

Bring a pot of salted water to a boil, add the pasta, and cook 1 minute less than the package instructions say, or until al dente.

Combine the onions, garlic, chile flakes, and oil in a saucepan over medium heat. Cook until the onions and garlic are soft but not colored, 2 to 3 minutes. Add the cuttlefish—take care that nothing burns or brown—and cook just until cooked through, probably about 1 minute. Add salt and pepper to taste. Drain the pasta and add to the pan, tossing to combine and heat the pasta through. Add the parsley and toss. Drizzle with olive oil and sprinkle the zest over the top.

Fava Bean Agnolotti with Snails and Herbed Butter

The classic French preparation for snails—bathed in puddles of garlic butter—formed the inspiration for this pasta. Although the agnolotti would be spectacular on their own, wearing only the barest of sauces, adding briny snails and a bright, intensely flavored compound butter makes the dish that much more special. You can find good-quality canned snails at European markets and some high-end grocery stores. Wait to make your sauce until the pasta is cooking; if you heat the butter too far ahead of time, the herbs might brown.

FILLING

1 cup shucked and skinned fava beans (about 2 pounds in the shell)

$^1/_2$ cup Fresh Ricotta (page 110)

$^1/_2$ cup freshly grated Parmigiano-Reggiano

Kosher salt

1 fresh egg yolk

1 tablespoon water

$^1/_2$ recipe Semolina Pasta (page 84)

1 recipe Compound Butter (recipe follows)

$^1/_2$ pound shelled snails

Kosher salt

Extra-virgin olive oil, for drizzling

To make the filling, combine the fava beans, ricotta, and grated cheese in a food processor until smooth. Season to taste with salt. Spoon the filling into a large pastry bag or a large resealable bag with one corner snipped off. Set aside.

Combine the egg yolk and water in a small bowl, beating lightly.

Divide the pasta dough in half. Roll out the pasta to make a 12 by 5-inch rectangle. Pipe a 1-inch-wide strip of filling down the long edge closest to you, $^1/_4$ inch in from the edge. Brush a 1-inch strip of egg wash next to the filling. Roll the pasta and filling up and away from you toward the opposing long edge so that the filling is completely enclosed in the pasta, pressing down to seal the filling inside. Brush a strip of egg wash alongside the enclosed filling and repeat. Using your thumbs or index fingers, press down firmly in 1-inch intervals along the log, pinching off the filling and pasta to form individual rectangles. Using a pastry cutter or sharp knife, trim excess pasta from the long edge, leaving a $^1/_2$-inch overhang. Cut between the agnolotti to separate them. Repeat using the rest of the filling and dough.

Bring a large pot of salted water to a boil. Add the agnolotti in batches to avoid crowding, and cook for 4 to 5 minutes, or until the pasta is cooked through and the filling is hot. While the pasta cooks, heat the herbed butter in a large sauté pan over medium-low heat and add the snails. Cook, stirring occasionally, for 2 to 3 minutes, or until the butter is melted and the snails are heated through. When the pasta is cooked, drain and add to the sauté pan with the snails and butter, along with a tablespoon or two of cooking water. Stir to coat the pasta with the butter. Season to taste with salt.

Divide among 4 plates, drizzle with olive oil, and serve.

COMPOUND BUTTER

Small bunch parsley, leaves removed

Small bunch chives, roughly chopped

3 cloves garlic, roughly chopped

$^1/_2$ cup unsalted butter, softened

Kosher salt

Combine all the ingredients in a blender or food processor and pulse until combined.

Gnocchetti with Pancetta, Chanterelles, and Mint

This was the very first recipe that we cooked for this book, and it remains a favorite. It's a perfect summer-into-fall pasta dish for when chanterelles are at their best. The gnocchetti are also a nice size for sharing.

Kosher salt and freshly ground pepper

$^1/_2$ pound dried gnocchetti sardi

$^3/_4$ pound fresh chanterelle mushrooms

2 tablespoons extra-virgin olive oil, plus more for drizzling

$^1/_2$ pound pancetta, cut into small dice

3 medium cloves garlic, thinly sliced

Pinch of chile flakes

2 tablespoons fresh mint, chopped

2 tablespoons fresh parsley, chopped

Parmigiano-Reggiano, for serving

Bring a large pot of lightly salted water to a rolling boil. Add the pasta and cook for about 12 minutes, or 1 minute less than the package directions.

While the pasta is cooking, clean the mushrooms and slice off the tough end of each stem. Quarter large mushrooms and halve the others. Any tiny chanterelles may be left whole. Set aside.

Heat the olive oil in a sauté pan over medium heat. Add the pancetta and sauté until some of the fat renders and the pancetta is golden, about 5 minutes. You don't want it to become too crisp. Add the mushrooms and sauté for 5 to 6 minutes, stirring occasionally to prevent sticking. When the mushrooms are golden, add the garlic and cook for 1 minute longer. Add the chile flakes.

When the pasta is ready, drain and add to the mushroom-pancetta mixture, adding a couple of tablespoons of cooking water if the mixture seems dry. Season with salt and pepper. Add the mint and parsley and toss.

Tip into a serving bowl. Drizzle with olive oil. Using a vegetable peeler, shave a few large curls of Parmigiano-Reggiano on top.

Tagliarini with Totten Virginica Oysters, Prosecco, Chives, and Cream

Think of this dish as the upscale cousin of that old standby, linguine with clams. Sparkling and oysters are a natural and festive combination, and here they combine to create a quick, fabulous pasta. This dish is almost a lighter version of an oyster stew, with the oysters poached just until done, the sauce brightened with prosecco, and then served over a fresh tangle of tagliarini. This would make a nice addition to a New Year's Eve menu, or make any winter supper feel like a holiday.

Kosher salt

16 Totten Virginica oysters in the shell
(use 6 per person if using a smaller oyster)

$^1/_2$ cup prosecco

4 tablespoons heavy cream

2 tablespoons unsalted butter

1 pound fresh tagliarini

4 tablespoons minced chives

Set a pot of water to boil over high heat and add a small handful of salt.

Shuck the oysters over a bowl to catch all their liquor. In a saucepan over high heat, combine the oyster liquor, prosecco, cream, and butter. Bring to a boil, then lower the heat and simmer until reduced by half. You should end up with $^1/_2$ to $^3/_4$ cup total liquid. Add the oysters and immediately turn off the heat, allowing the residual heat to gently poach the oysters while the pasta cooks.

Add the pasta to the boiling water and cook for 2 to 3 minutes. Drain and add to the sauce. Add the chives, toss, and taste for seasoning. Serve in warmed bowls.

Maloreddus with Squid, Tomato Sauce, and Lemon

Maloreddus are delicate, saffron-infused pasta with a lovely golden hue and a hint of warmth from the saffron. They are especially good paired with fish or seafood, and lend themselves well to sweet and sour combinations, like this dish featuring a light, fresh tomato sauce accented with lemon and briny olives. You can find maloreddus in Italian specialty stores or through online sources.

8 ounces dried maloreddus

1 lemon

2 cups Basic Tomato Sauce (page 216)

1 pound fresh squid, cleaned and sliced into ribbons

1 cup pitted, chopped Taggiasca olives

Kosher salt and freshly ground pepper

Extra-virgin olive oil, for drizzling

Bring a large pot of salted water to a boil. Add the pasta and cook for 1 minute less than the package directions say.

Remove the zest from the lemon with a fine grater. Cut the lemon in half.

While the pasta is cooking, heat the sauce in a high-sided pan over medium heat. When the sauce reaches a simmer, add the squid and cook for 2 to 3 minutes, or just until opaque. Do not overcook.

When the pasta is done, drain and tip into the pan with the sauce. Add the olives, juice of half the lemon, and salt and pepper to taste.

Divide among 4 shallow bowls. Sprinkle the lemon zest over the top, drizzle with olive oil, and serve.

Spaghetti with Garlic, Chile, and Sea Urchin

Creamy, rich sea urchin roe—better known by sushi lovers as "uni"—makes one of the most extraordinary sauces for pasta that I know, exotic Italian comfort food. We serve different versions in the restaurants, but this is my favorite because it keeps the roe intact. The heat of the pasta "cooks" the roe and each sac is broken only by your fork, allowing you to control the richness of each bite. If you do not have access to live sea urchin, make sure the roe you buy is brightly colored and smells like the sea. For the very best flavor and texture, seek out small-production, artisanal pasta, available in Italian import shops and food stores.

Kosher salt

2 live sea urchins, or 4 ounces sea urchin roe

1 pound dried linguine

$1/2$ cup extra-virgin olive oil

2 cloves garlic, thinly sliced

1 teaspoon chile flakes

1 bunch Italian parsley, leaves removed from stems and finely chopped

Set a pot of water to boil over high heat. Add a small handful of salt.

If using live sea urchin, hold a sea urchin in one hand, protecting it with a kitchen towel. Using utility shears, cut the top off the sea urchin and discard. Rinse the inside of the urchin gently with cool water. Using a spoon, scoop out each of the five yellow sacs inside, placing them in a bowl of water as you remove them. Repeat with the second sea urchin. Gently swish the sacs in the water to remove any blood, then gently remove and set to dry on paper towels.

When the water has come to a rolling boil, add the pasta and stir to separate. Cook until slightly firmer than al dente, about 10 minutes, or 1 minute less than the package directions.

In a sauté pan over medium heat, warm the olive oil with the garlic and chile flakes for 2 to 3 minutes, until the garlic softens but does not color. When the pasta is cooked, drain well, then add to the sauté pan and toss. Increase the heat to medium-high, add the sea urchins, and toss gently, trying to keep the sacs as intact as possible. Add the parsley and toss again gently. Divide among 4 deep bowls and serve immediately.

Trofie with Nettle Pesto

Trofie, also called trofiette, is a Ligurian pasta made with just flour and water—no eggs. The squiggly little twists make a particularly good vehicle for pesto because it nestles into all those little crevices. The Nettle Pesto is lighter and less herbaceous than traditional basil pesto, making this an easy first course.

Kosher salt

12 ounces dried trofie

1/2 cup Nettle Pesto (recipe follows)

Grated Parmigiano-Reggiano, for serving

Set a pot of water to boil over high heat. Add a small handful of salt. Add the trofie and cook for 1 minute less than the package directions say. Drain and reserve the cooking liquid.

Toss the pasta with the pesto and 1/4 cup reserved pasta water. Divide among 4 shallow bowls and top each serving with a little grated Parmigiano-Reggiano.

NETTLE PESTO

Kosher salt

4 ounces fresh nettle tips

3 cloves garlic

3/4 cup pine nuts

1 cup extra-virgin olive oil

1 cup grated Parmigiano-Reggiano

Bring a pot of salted water to a boil and prepare an ice bath. Add the nettles to the boiling water and cook for 3 minutes, then plunge immediately into the ice bath to stop the cooking. Remove the nettles and squeeze very dry. Chop finely.

Combine the nettles with the garlic, pine nuts, and a pinch of salt in a food processor. Pulse to combine. Add the oil in a steady stream until you have a uniform, thick paste. Transfer to a bowl and stir in the cheese.

This recipe makes much more than you'll need to serve four. If you top the pesto with a sealing layer of olive oil, it should last for 2 or 3 days in the fridge.

Pappardelle with Tomato Sauce and Marinated Pecorino Sardo

This may be one of the simplest recipes in this entire book, but it's absolutely addictive, with the marinated pecorino offering a tangy creaminess that coats the silky noodles just so. Don't be tempted to jazz this up with anything extra—it's the comforting straightforwardness of the dish that makes it so good. Trying to make it fancy will ruin the magic.

2 cups Basic Tomato Sauce (page 216)

$1/2$ pound Preserved Pecorino Sardo (page 218)

Kosher salt and freshly ground pepper

1 pound fresh semolina pappardelle (page 84)

In a sauté pan over medium-low heat, bring the tomato sauce to a simmer. Finely crumble the cheese into the sauce, allowing it to melt and incorporate.

Bring a large pot of salted water to a boil. Add the pasta and cook for 2 to 3 minutes, or until just al dente.

When the pasta is ready, drain and tip into the pan with the sauce. Season with salt and pepper, toss, and serve immediately.

Bigoli with Grilled Sardines and Fennel

If you were Venetian, and therefore Catholic, and were forbidden to eat meat on Fridays, you might choose instead a delicious whole wheat pasta tossed with rich sardines and fennel for your supper. Aren't you lucky, then, that even if you are a Swedish Lutheran, you can happily take part in this lovely ritual? Bigoli is yummy fresh, but it can also be found dried in Italian markets. Although you could substitute other types of pasta, the depth of flavor of the whole wheat really holds up to the intensity of the fish.

Kosher salt and freshly ground pepper

1 pound bigoli

1/2 cup extra-virgin olive oil, plus more for brushing

3 cloves garlic, thinly sliced

1 teaspoon chile flakes

12 sardines, scaled and gutted

4 tablespoons chopped fennel fronds

Bring a large pot of salted water to a boil. Add the pasta and cook for 1 minute less than the package directions say.

While the pasta is cooking, heat the olive oil, garlic, and chile flakes in a large sauté pan over medium-low heat. Cook gently, stirring occasionally, for 2 to 3 minutes, until the garlic is soft but not brown.

Brush the sardines with olive oil and season with salt and pepper on both sides and in the cavity. Heat a grill pan on high. Add the sardines and grill for 2 minutes on each side, or until just done. When the fish are cool enough to handle, pull the meat off the bones in large chunks and add to a bowl. Add the fennel, toss, and reserve.

Drain the bigoli and tip into the pan with the infused oil. Toss to coat, and then divide among 4 shallow bowls. Spoon any remaining oil over the fish and fennel and toss gently. Spoon the fish over the pasta and serve.

Duck Egg Ravioli with Ricotta and Swiss Chard

You know that friend who calls himself a "foodie," who isn't impressed with anything you make, because, yawn, he's made it before and then took it molecular? Make him eat his words with ravioli stuffed with tender chard, rich ricotta, and—this is the magic part—a duck egg that stays intact until the ravioli is cut, releasing a luscious river of yolk. These are big and rich; two per person is plenty.

FILLING

1 bunch Swiss chard

1 tablespoon unsalted butter

1¹/₂ cups ricotta

1 clove garlic, minced

Kosher salt and freshly ground pepper

¹/₂ recipe Egg Pasta (page 84)

8 duck egg yolks, at room temperature

3 tablespoons unsalted butter

Parmigiano-Reggiano, for serving

To make the filling, wash and stem the Swiss chard, then roughly chop it. Heat the butter in a sauté pan over medium-high heat and add the chard, stirring until wilted. Allow to cool, then squeeze dry and combine with the ricotta and garlic; season to taste with salt and pepper. Set aside while you roll out the pasta.

Roll out the dough to the thinnest setting on your pasta machine. Cut the pasta sheet in half crosswise so that you have 4 rectangles about 18 inches long. Dust your work surface with flour, then lay out one strip of pasta. Dollop about 2 tablespoons of the ricotta-chard mixture every 3 inches, making 4 servings. Make a slight depression in each dollop of filling, then gently place one egg yolk in each depression. Brush the surrounding pasta dough with water, then cover the filling with the second sheet of pasta. Use the edges of your hands to press down around the filling, pressing out any air and sealing the dough. Cut out the ravioli using a biscuit cutter or drinking glass. Repeat with the remaining pasta sheets, filling, and yolks to make 4 more ravioli.

Fill 2 high-sided pans with 2 inches of water and bring to a bare simmer. Slip the ravioli into the water and poach gently, adjusting the heat to maintain a bare simmer. Cook the ravioli for about 2¹/₂ minutes, or just until the pasta is cooked and the filling is heated through. It's important that you don't overcook the ravioli so that the yolks stay liquid. Reserve the pasta water.

Melt the butter in a wide pan, add the pasta cooking liquid, and swirl together to combine. Add the ravioli to the pan and gently spoon the sauce over to coat. Divide among 4 shallow bowls, and top with a bit of sauce. Shave the Parmigiano-Reggiano over the top and serve.

Switch-Hitting Clams with Ramps

I wouldn't hazard a guess as to the romantic preferences of clams. What I do know is that this dish works equally well served as a substantial soup or as a brothy pasta, depending on your own desires. I use jumbo clams in this dish because they have a more pronounced flavor. They are a bit chewier, but I think the improved flavor is worth a small sacrifice in terms of texture. For the pasta, this is where you get to have some fun. Use a ridged pastry wheel if you want your squares to be extra elegant, or haul out a sharp knife if you want basic squares. Either way, they'll taste delicious.

12 ounces fresh Semolina Pasta sheets (page 84)

Kosher salt

4 pounds jumbo clams

3 cloves garlic, sliced paper-thin

Juice of $1/2$ lemon

1 cup white wine

2 tablespoons extra-virgin olive oil

8 ramps, thinly sliced

Cut the pasta sheets into $1/2$-inch strips with a knife or pastry wheel. Cut at $1/2$-inch intervals to form $1/2$-inch squares. Set a large pot of salted water on the stove to boil.

In a large pot with a lid, combine the clams, garlic, lemon juice, and wine. Cover, place over high heat, and bring to a boil. Steam the clams just until they open—no more than a few minutes after the liquid has come to a boil. This ensures they will stay tender. Discard any clams that fail to open. When cool enough to handle, remove the clams from their shells and reserve them in their liquid.

Add the pasta to the boiling water and cook for 2 to 3 minutes, or until just al dente.

While the pasta cooks, heat the olive oil in a sauté pan over medium-high heat and sauté the ramps until soft, 2 to 3 minutes. Add the clams and their liquid, then drain the pasta and add to the pan; swirl to combine. Serve in deep, warmed bowls.

Cannelloni with Braised Pork Cheeks and Sweet Cicely

Cannelloni, you say? Isn't that the type of old-school Italian food you order at places with red-and-white checked tablecloths and candles stuck into Chianti bottles? Well, yes, and no. For this dish, you first braise some succulent pork cheeks until they shred when you look at them. Then you create a rich, savory broth that you use to moisten the pork, and accent it with sweet cicely, an herb with an aniselike flavor. Roll it in silken squares of pasta and coat with Parmigiano-Reggiano and cream. Sometimes old school is worth resurrecting.

FILLING

2 pounds pork cheeks (trimmed of any excess fat and sinew)

Kosher salt and freshly ground pepper

4 tablespoons extra-virgin olive oil, plus more for drizzling

2 carrots, peeled and roughly chopped

4 cloves garlic, smashed

1 onion, chopped

1 cup white wine

3 cups Prosciutto Broth (page 47)

2 fresh bay leaves

3 tablespoons minced sweet cicely or chervil

CANNELLONI

1/2 recipe Egg Pasta (page 84)

2 tablespoons unsalted butter, diced

1 cup grated Parmigiano-Reggiano

Extra-virgin olive oil, for drizzling

Preheat the oven to 350°F.

To make the filling, season the pork liberally with salt and pepper on both sides. Using 2 sauté pans to avoid crowding, heat 2 tablespoons olive oil in each pan over high heat. Sear the pork cheeks for 2 to 3 minutes per side, or until nicely caramelized.

Transfer the meat to a braising dish. Divide the carrots, garlic, and onion between the pans and sauté just until they get a hint of color, 2 to 3 minutes. Deglaze the pans with the wine, scraping up any crusty bits. Put the vegetables and wine into the braising dish with the pork cheeks, then pour in the broth and add the bay leaves. Cover the dish with foil or a heavy, tight-fitting lid and braise for 3 hours, or until the meat shreds easily with a fork.

Remove the meat from the braising dish and shred with two forks. Add the sweet cicely and season to taste with salt and pepper. Add a couple of spoonfuls of braising liquid and drizzle with olive oil to moisten. Stir to combine and set aside. Strain the braising liquid into a clean pan and reduce by half; the timing will vary depending on your stove and pan, but will be about 15 to 20 minutes.

Preheat the oven to 350°F.

To make the cannelloni, roll out the pasta dough to #2 thickness. Using a pastry wheel and a ruler, trim the rolled-out sheets to measure 5 inches across. Then cut the sheets horizontally to create 5-inch squares. You should end up with 8 pasta squares in all.

Using a 13 by 9-inch baking dish, spoon enough reduced braising liquid to cover the bottom. Place about 3 table-spoons of the pork filling along one edge of a pasta square. Roll up to encase the filling and form a cylinder, then place seam-side down in the baking dish. Repeat with the remaining pasta squares and filling. Sprinkle the diced butter over the top of the dish and then sprinkle with the cheese.

Cover the dish tightly with foil. Bake for 30 minutes. Increase the heat to 400°F and remove the foil. Bake for 10 minutes longer, or until the cheese browns and bubbles. Remove the dish from the oven and drizzle with the olive oil. Let cool for 5 minutes before serving.

Something Foraged, Something Green: Salads, Vegetables, and Sides

One of the best parts of the back-to-the-farm craze that has hit this country is that vegetables are finally getting their due. Read a modern menu and it's not just your meat or fish that is featured, but also the sides and salads, some of the names reading like poetry. And poetry is an apt metaphor for a range of foods that, in season, offer jewel tones, concentrated flavor, and textures that dance on your tongue.

As with all of the recipes in this book, the key lies in choosing your vegetables with care, using only the freshest, youngest offerings and shopping in season. No matter how well you prepare it, serving a shaved artichoke in the dead of winter is an affront, to the vegetable and to your guests. Instead, why not choose a salad that mingles sweet Cara Cara oranges with olives and shallot? The flavor and color is what the season calls for; cooking in season is always preferable to trying to force a dish for the sake of a preconceived menu.

Some of the dishes offered in this section are substantial enough to stand in for meals. Seared Rabbit Loin with Frisée and Pancetta falls into this category, as does Panzanella with Crispy Pig's Ear. Others, such as Puntarelle with Anchovy, Garlic, and Parsley Dressing or Lentils with Pancetta, can stand alone as a plate in a multicourse meal, or nestle up to meat or fish as a side.

Whether you serve these dishes as sides or stand-alone plates, pay attention to texture as well as taste. A shaved radish falls differently on the tongue than a thick slice; peas and favas should always retain a bit of their snap. Perhaps the dishes I am most fussy about are the salads. Please wash and dry your greens with care—nothing ruins a salad more quickly than a bite of sand or grit. Likewise, use only the most tender tips and leaves from your greens, whether it's arugula or watercress. You will be rewarded with dishes that succeed beyond measure and that deserve a place in the center, not the side, of the plate.

Baby Beet Salad with Fresh Ricotta

Baby beets shine like tender jewels in this salad, their color offset by creamy, handmade ricotta. Roasting the beets heightens the sweetness, concentrating their flavor, while the orange adds a touch of brightness. I use baby arugula and watercress here, though you can choose any other baby greens that have a little bite to them.

1 pound baby beets

1 orange, quartered

3 sprigs fresh thyme, leaves removed

1/2 cup extra-virgin olive oil

4 bunches spring radishes, trimmed

1 bunch watercress

1 bunch baby arugula

Kosher salt

1 cup Fresh Ricotta (recipe follows)

Aged balsamic vinegar, for drizzling

Preheat the oven to 350°F.

Wash the beets and remove the greens. Trim the root ends. Toss the beets with the orange sections and thyme leaves and drizzle with 1 tablespoon olive oil. Wrap tightly in foil and roast for about 1 hour, or until tender. When cool enough to handle, peel the beets and halve them. Discard the oranges and thyme. Sprinkle the cooked beets with salt and toss with 2 tablespoons olive oil.

Thinly slice the radishes with a chef's knife or mandoline. Pick over the watercress and arugula, choosing only the best, most tender tips. Toss with the radishes. Dress the watercress salad with 3 tablespoons of the olive oil and sprinkle with salt.

Add a pinch or two of salt and 2 tablespoons olive oil to the ricotta. Stir until smooth and creamy.

Set out 4 plates and smear 2 tablespoons ricotta in a stripe down the middle of each. Arrange the beets on top of the ricotta. Drizzle with the remaining olive oil and 1 teaspoon of aged balsamic per plate. Divide the watercress salad into 4 portions and place to the side of the beets on the plate.

FRESH RICOTTA

4 cups whole milk

1 cup buttermilk

Line a fine-mesh sieve with a double layer of cheesecloth and set in a sink or over a bowl.

Combine the milk and buttermilk in a large saucepan or enameled pot. Heat very slowly over low heat until the mixture reaches 165°F. The mixture will begin to curdle, literally separating into thick curds and whey, a thin liquid. Use a slotted spoon to remove the curds to the lined sieve. Allow to drain and set for 30 to 45 minutes, or until thick.

Endive Salad with Creamy Meyer Lemon Vinaigrette

This lovely salad can slide from late winter into early spring when bouquets of radishes proliferate in the market. Some people find endive too harsh, but here the flavor is mellowed a bit and the leaves are given extra snap by a saltwater soak. This is a study in textures, with the silky endive accented by the crunch of the nuts, all lightly bound with a tart but delicate Meyer lemon dressing. Because of the egg yolk, the vinaigrette won't last for more than two days in the fridge, but you'll find lots of uses for any leftover dressing. Try tossing it with boiled Piccolo potatoes or use it on your favorite greens.

4 heads Belgian endive, outer leaves trimmed and quartered

3 Meyer lemons

2 tablespoons water

1 fresh egg yolk

1 teaspoon Dijon mustard

Kosher salt

$1/2$ cup extra-virgin olive oil

$1/2$ cup canola oil

$1/2$ cup toasted pistachios

$1/2$ bunch Italian parsley, leaves picked

3 or 4 radishes, trimmed

Remove the outer leaves from the endive and trim any stems, taking care to keep the heads intact. Cut each head lengthwise into quarters. To remove some of the bitterness, soak the endives in lightly salted ice water for 10 minutes. Remove and let drain on paper towels.

Peel strips of zest from one of the lemons with a vegetable peeler. Place the zest with a couple of inches of water in a small saucepan. Bring to a boil, drain the water, then replace the water with fresh, cold water. Repeat the entire process three times—don't cheat! Blanching the zest three times removes any traces of bitterness and guarantees a softer, more floral vinaigrette.

Juice the lemons for a total of $1/4$ cup. In the jar of a blender, combine the juice with the blanched zest, the water, egg yolk, mustard, and a pinch of salt. Pulse to chop the ingredients. Then add both oils in a slow, steady stream. Strain the vinaigrette to remove any large pieces of zest. You should end up with about $1 1/2$ cups of dressing.

Place the endives, nuts, and parsley in a bowl and toss with enough dressing to lightly coat. Pile on a platter, then shave the radishes over the top of the salad and serve.

Seared Rabbit Loin with Frisée and Pancetta

This is a very grown-up salad and my idea of a fantastic lunch. It also happens to be a great way to use loins left over when you've braised or stewed the richer, darker pieces of your rabbit. Like pork tenderloin or filet mignon, rabbit loin can't take that sort of cooking. Give it a quick sear instead, and toss it with crisp pancetta and frisée in a Chianti vinaigrette. You'll find yourself making rabbit more often just to end up with spare loins.

3 heads frisée

4 ounces pancetta, diced

4 rabbit loins (from 2 rabbits)

7 tablespoons extra-virgin olive oil

2 tablespoons Chianti vinegar

2 heaping tablespoons pitted Luccino olives

1 shallot, minced

Kosher salt and freshly ground pepper

To prepare the frisée, remove the outer green leaves, reserving only the soft yellow inner part of each head. Separate the leaves, rinse well, and dry.

Cook the pancetta in a sauté pan over medium heat until it crisps and the fat renders, 3 to 4 minutes. Drain and reserve.

Trim the loins of any connective tissue. Heat 3 tablespoons of the olive oil in a sauté pan over high heat. Add the loins and brown well on all sides. Transfer the loins to a plate to rest, then slice $1/2$ inch thick.

Combine the vinegar, the remaining 4 tablespoons olive oil, the olives, and the shallot in a bowl. Add the frisée, sliced rabbit loin, and pancetta. Toss gently to combine and season with salt and pepper. Divide among 4 small plates and serve.

Lentils with Pancetta

Most recipes for basic lentils call for you to cook the legumes with vegetables until the lentils are tender. In the restaurants, we precook the lentils with celery, onions, and garlic, then finish the dish with finely diced vegetables that keep their flavor and texture, adding pancetta for richness and texture. I'm sure that once you try this technique, you won't go back to the mushy mélange that home cooks usually end up with. The lentils make a nice accompaniment to fish and poultry entrées.

LENTILS

2 stalks celery, cut in half

1 onion, peeled and halved horizontally

2 cloves garlic

$1/2$ cup lentils

2 tablespoons unsalted butter

6 ounces pancetta, diced (about 1 cup)

$1/2$ cup finely diced carrot

$1/2$ cup finely diced celery

$1/2$ cup finely diced shallot

3 cloves garlic, sliced

3 tablespoons chopped fresh parsley

2 tablespoons extra-virgin olive oil

To make the lentils, place all the ingredients in a deep saucepan and cover with 1 inch of water. Bring to a boil over high heat, then reduce the heat to low and simmer for 20 to 25 minutes, or until the lentils are al dente. Discard the vegetables. Pour the lentils and their liquid into a bowl and place in the refrigerator to cool. When cooled, strain the lentils, reserving 1 cup of the liquid.

Heat the butter in a sauté pan over medium heat and add the pancetta. Render the fat from the pancetta and saute until slightly crisp, 3 to 4 minutes. Add the carrots, celery, shallot, and garlic and cook until tender, an additional 3 to 4 minutes. Add the lentils and the reserved cooking liquid, then bring to a boil. Turn off the heat, stir in the parsley and olive oil, and taste for seasoning. Serve hot.

Fried Cauliflower with Ham Hock

SERVES 4

Cauliflower is another one of those vegetables that gets a bad rap. Yes, it's in the cabbage family, and when the cauliflower is raw, the connection is easy to identify. Take a page from the Italians, then, who aren't afraid of oil and know that giving some vegetables a dip in the fryer brings out their best characteristics. In this case, the cauliflower turns sweet and silken; add in some smoky shreds of ham hock and, well, you'll be begging to eat cauliflower more often. Ask your butcher to split the ham hock for you; they have big saws for that very purpose. And don't you dare throw away the liquid left over from boiling the ham hock. One bonus of this recipe is a soup waiting to happen.

1 smoked ham hock, split in half

1 head cauliflower

2 cups extra-virgin olive oil

Kosher salt and freshly ground pepper

Place the ham hock in a deep pot and cover with cold water by 1 inch. Place over medium-high heat and boil for 2 to $2^1/_2$ hours, until the meat nearly falls off the bone. Remove the meat from what is now a delicious broth and transfer to a plate to cool. Reserve the broth for another use. When the meat has cooled enough to handle, shred the meat from the bone into bite-size pieces, removing and discarding any fat and tendon as you go. You should end up with about $1^1/_2$ cups of picked meat, depending on the size of the ham hock. Measure out 1 packed cup of meat and wrap in foil to keep warm. Reserve the rest for another dish.

To prepare the cauliflower, trim the stalk. Break into small florets of even size—no bigger than $1^1/_2$ inches long, with stems no thicker than a pencil.

Heat the olive oil in a heavy, deep saucepan fitted with a frying thermometer. When the oil reaches 350°F, shallow-fry the cauliflower in batches until golden brown, 4 to 6 minutes. Drain the fried cauliflower on paper towels and transfer to a warmed bowl. Work quickly so that the cauliflower stays hot. When all the cauliflower is fried, add the shredded ham hock, season with salt and pepper, and serve.

116   ETHAN STOWELL'S NEW ITALIAN KITCHEN

Lobster Mushrooms with Preserved Garlic, Parsley, and Oregano

Lobster mushrooms are named for their gorgeous color and appear in Northwest markets from August through October. They have a delicate flavor and are very fine textured, making them a lovely addition to the plate.

The preserved garlic ties the whole dish together, so don't be tempted to substitute fresh. Not only would the taste be too harsh for this delicate mushroom, but you'd also miss the mellow richness the preserved garlic offers. If you can't find lobster mushrooms, you can use other wild mushrooms such as chanterelles or hedgehogs, though the flavor will be different.

3/4 pound lobster mushrooms

4 ounces pancetta, diced

12 cloves Preserved Garlic (page 217)

Kosher salt and freshly ground pepper

1 tablespoon chopped fresh parsley

1 tablespoon chopped fresh oregano

Extra-virgin olive oil, for drizzling

Fill a bowl with cool water. Plunge the mushrooms into the water and remove immediately to paper towels to drain. Trim the stem ends, then halve any large pieces. Allow the mushrooms to air-dry while you cook the pancetta.

Cook the pancetta in a sauté pan over medium heat for 4 to 5 minutes, or until some of the fat has rendered. Add the mushrooms and garlic. You will see the mushrooms release their liquid, then start to sizzle as the liquid begins to evaporate, 6 to 8 minutes. Season to taste with salt and pepper.

Just before serving, add the parsley and oregano and toss. Drizzle with olive oil and serve immediately.

Shaved Artichoke and Wild Watercress Salad

Wild watercress appears sporadically in farmers' markets, but it also grows in more places than you might think. In Seattle, it's positively thick around Lake Washington and easy to find and pick. Whether you forage for your own or buy it from a purveyor, make sure you pick or buy more than you think you'll need. I like to use only the very freshest tips and bits for the salad. The peppery flavor is a nice contrast to the mild, grassy flavor of the pecorino and marries well with the earthy finish of the artichokes.

2 large artichokes

1 lemon, halved

Kosher salt and freshly ground pepper

8 cups loosely packed wild watercress tips

$1/4$ cup extra-virgin olive oil

Pecorino Toscano, for serving

To prepare the artichokes, first peel the fibrous outer covering from the stems, trimming only the very bottom and leaving as much stem intact as possible. (See step-by-step photos on pages 16 and 17.) Cut off the top of each artichoke with a very sharp chef's knife. Next, pull off all the tough outer leaves. Use kitchen shears to snip off the tops of the tender inner leaves. Quarter the artichoke and remove the choke from each quarter. Shave each quarter using a mandoline. Immediately put the slices in a bowl, squeeze $1/2$ lemon over, and toss. This will keep the slices from turning brown. Season with salt and pepper.

Add the cress to the bowl. Drizzle the olive oil over the top and squeeze the other lemon half over the salad. Gently toss.

Divide the salad among 4 plates, ensuring each portion contains the same amount of artichoke. Shave the cheese over the top of each and serve.

Blood Orange Salad with Shallot and Taggiasca Olives

SERVES 4

This salad is a stellar addition to a midwinter antipasto plate, full of bright flavors that seem to hint at warmer days ahead. In the short, dark days of a Seattle January, that's especially welcome.

Because of the salad's simplicity, it's important to use the heaviest, sweetest oranges you can find and use a firm, briny olive. Arbequinas or Gaetas are fine substitutes for the Taggiascas; mushy supermarket Kalamatas are not. Serve the salad shortly after you prepare it. As it sits, the flavor of the shallot continues to develop and the lovely balance of the salad is lost.

2 blood oranges

2 Cara Cara oranges

2 small shallots, or $^1/_4$ small red onion

$^1/_2$ cup pitted Taggiasca olives

$^1/_4$ cup best-quality olive oil

Cut the top and bottom off each orange. Using a sharp knife, slice down between the pith and the flesh of the orange, following the curve of the fruit. Repeat until all the peel and pith is removed. Slice crosswise and remove any seeds. Arrange the slices on a platter.

Using a mandoline or a very sharp knife, slice the shallots into paper-thin rings. Separate and scatter over the orange slices. Garnish the salad with the olives and drizzle with the olive oil. Serve immediately.

Rapini with Garlic, Chile, and Lemon

You may know rapini as broccoli rabe, that delightfully bitter green you see in the market next to its mild cousin, chard. Blanching the rapini first tames a bit of the bitterness, while the straightforward preparation allows the vegetable to still be its bold self. Serve with roasted or grilled meats, dishes with assertive flavors that will hold up to the greens.

2 bunches rapini

3 tablespoons extra-virgin olive oil

3 cloves garlic, thinly sliced

Pinch of chile flakes

Kosher salt and freshly ground pepper

1/2 lemon

Wash the greens carefully, plunging each leaf in plenty of cold water and swishing to loosen any dirt or grit. Remove the soft leaves from the tough stems and set aside. Bring a large pot of salted water to a rapid boil. While the water is heating, prepare an ice-water bath to shock the rapini and stop the cooking. When the water has come to a boil, add the rapini and blanch just long enough to set the color and tame the bitterness, not longer than 1 minute. Immediately plunge into the ice bath. When cool, drain the rapini and squeeze dry. Set aside.

Heat the oil in a sauté pan over medium-low heat and add the garlic and chile flakes, allowing them to infuse the oil. Keep the heat low enough that the garlic doesn't color. Add the blanched greens and sauté until the rapini is warmed through but still a little crunchy. Season with salt and pepper, squeeze the lemon over the greens, and serve.

Delicata Squash with Chestnut Honey

In this fabulous early-winter side, roasted delicata is caramelized in the oven and accented with the assertive flavor of dark amber chestnut honey. Delicata is a striped, hard-shelled heirloom squash that trades flavor for trans-portability. Unlike butternut or kabocha, delicata can be cooked and eaten with the peel intact. You can substitute other types of winter squash in this recipe, just make sure you peel them first and vary the cooking time accordingly.

2 delicata squash, 1 to 1¹/₂ pounds in all

2 tablespoons extra-virgin olive oil

Kosher salt and freshly ground pepper

2 tablespoons Tuscan chestnut honey

2 tablespoons unsalted butter

Preheat the oven to 375°F.

Cut off the ends of each squash and split lengthwise. Scoop out the seeds with a spoon. Cut each half horizontally into $^3/_4$- to 1-inch slices. The slices should resemble half-moons.

Divide the olive oil between 2 sauté pans large enough to hold the squash in a single layer. Heat the pans over high heat until the oil is almost smoking. Brown the squash on both sides until deep golden brown, 3 to 4 minutes per side.

Transfer the squash to paper towels to drain. While still hot, season with salt and pepper.

Arrange the squash in a single layer in a small baking dish, drizzle with the honey, and dot with the butter. Bake for 15 to 20 minutes to finish cooking the squash and heat through.

Note: The dish can be prepared up to the point of putting the dish in the oven. The squash can sit on the counter for a few hours before baking, while you finish cooking the rest of the meal.

Puntarelle with Anchovy, Garlic, and Parsley Dressing

Puntarelle is also called Catalonian chicory, though I think of it as a truly Italian vegetable. It is in the chicory family, with thicker stalks tapering to serrated leaves that look a bit like those of a dandelion. The leaves have a little bite to them, with more of a fennel-endive thing going on in the stalks. It might take some searching to find it in the market—you could always try asking your market if they would order it—but it's worth seeking out. In Rome, puntarelle is traditionally paired with strong flavors such as anchovy and garlic that can match the strong flavor of the vegetable, as I do here, along with an ice-water soak that takes off some of the edge. If you can't find puntarelle, I suppose you could substitute frisée, but then you're kind of missing the magic.

2 heads puntarelle

6 sprigs parsley

1 clove garlic

6 to 8 anchovy fillets, to taste, rinsed if packed in salt

1/4 cup extra-virgin olive oil

Juice of 1 lemon

Freshly cracked pepper

Parmigiano-Reggiano, for serving

To prepare the puntarelle, pull off the funky leaves and trim the ends of the stalks. Quarter the bigger stalks and slice the smaller stalks in half. Soak in ice water for about 1 hour. The leaves will crisp and curl. Drain.

Put the parsley, garlic, and anchovy fillets on your cutting board and chop them all together fairly finely with your knife. If you have a mortar and pestle, now would be a great time to use it, and it might make you feel like you were in Rome. Place in a bowl and whisk together with the oil and lemon juice.

Add freshly cracked pepper to the puntarelle, then toss with enough dressing to coat. Let it marinate for a couple of minutes, then taste for seasoning. Mound the salad on a plate and shave large strips of Parmigiano on top with a vegetable peeler. Serve.

Pickled Mackerel Salad with Watercress, Radish, and Pistachio

This delicious salad makes a solid first course or a hearty addition to a small-plate menu. Mackerel is a fantastic fish, with rich flesh and a deep flavor that is tamed and enhanced by a quick pickling treatment. Crisp radishes and assertive watercress hold up to the forward flavors, while a sprinkling of toasted pistachios adds nice texture and crunch. For a fun variation, use the same pickling liquid on sardines. Because sardine fillets are much thinner, they can be cooked simply by heating the liquid to boiling and pouring it over the fillets. Continue as directed with the rest of the recipe.

PICKLED MACKEREL

1 pound mackerel fillets

1 carrot, peeled and cut into coins

2 cloves garlic, sliced

1 small red onion, peeled and thinly sliced

1 cup white vinegar

1 cup water

2 tablespoons black peppercorns

1 tablespoon coriander seeds

1 tablespoon mustard seeds

3 fresh bay leaves

SALAD

2 bunches watercress

1 bunch radishes

1 shallot, thinly sliced

$1/4$ cup toasted pistachios

Kosher salt and freshly cracked pepper

$1^1/_2$ tablespoons extra-virgin olive oil

To make the mackerel, prepare the fish by removing any bones with tweezers. Remove the skin by laying the fillet, skin-side down, on your work surface. Insert a sharp knife between the skin and flesh. Grasping the skin with your fingers, gently saw the knife back and forth, keeping it parallel to the cutting board. Discard the bones and skin. You should end up with about $3/4$ pound trimmed fish.

In a large nonreactive saucepan over high heat, combine the carrot, garlic, onion, vinegar, water, and spices. Bring to a boil, then lower the heat and simmer for 5 minutes to blend the flavors. Decrease the heat to maintain a bare simmer, add the fish, and poach until just cooked through, 6 to 8 minutes. Pour the fish and the liquid into a nonreactive container (glass is best) and allow to cool for 10 minutes. For best flavor, refrigerate overnight, though the fish can be used as soon as it has cooled. When ready to use the fish, remove from the liquid and flake into large chunks. Reserve 2 tablespoons of the pickling liquid for use in the salad and discard the rest.

To make the salad, wash and dry the watercress, then pick off the tenderest leaves and place in a large bowl. Trim and thinly slice the radishes and add to the bowl, along with the shallot, nuts, and fish. Season to taste with salt and cracked pepper. Combine the olive oil and reserved pickling liquid, then add to the bowl and toss the mixture gently so as not to break up the fish. Divide among 4 plates and serve.

Roasted Fingerling Potatoes and Artichokes with Garlic and Thyme

This dish is one of the simple joys that comes from freshly dug new potatoes and the inimitable artichoke. You need nothing more than garlic and a hit of thyme to create a side that totally speaks of the earth and that would make even a simple grilled steak sublime.

1 pound fingerling potatoes

8 cloves garlic

2 tablespoons unsalted butter

2 tablespoons extra-virgin olive oil

2 artichokes, trimmed (see pages 16 and 17)

1/2 bunch thyme

Kosher salt and freshly ground pepper

Preheat the oven to 400°F.

Halve the potatoes lengthwise. Peel and halve the garlic cloves.

Heat the butter and oil together in a large, ovenproof sauté pan over medium-high heat. Add the potatoes, cut-side down, in a single layer. Cook until the potatoes are golden, 4 to 5 minutes.

Turn the potatoes and add the artichokes, cut-side down. Nestle the garlic and thyme amid the vegetables. Pop into the oven and roast until the artichokes and potatoes are tender, 10 to 12 minutes. Season to taste with salt and pepper and serve.

Company Alligator Pear

For those of you not familiar with the term, "alligator pear" is a charming and old-fashioned name for avocado. I use the term here because this is less a recipe than a memory. When I was growing up, my parents thought it the height of sophistication to serve us halved avocados as an accompaniment to our after-dinner salad. They filled them with olive oil and sprinkled them with salt and never failed to mention how rare and expensive a treat we were getting.

This is an homage to that family dinner tradition— half an alligator pear, made lighter and more savory with the addition of buttery Ligurian Taggiasca olives and a lightly dressed arugula salad. Serve them the next time you entertain and raise a fork to the Stowells as you do.

2 large, firm-ripe avocados

Kosher salt

4 tablespoons chopped pitted Taggiasca olives packed in oil

1 serrano chile, sliced

1 large lemon, halved

2 cups baby arugula

$1^1/_2$ tablespoons extra-virgin olive oil

Cut each avocado in half, remove the pits, and place each half on a salad plate. Sprinkle each half lightly with salt and fill each cavity with 1 tablespoon chopped olives and a bit of the oil in which they are packed. Sprinkle evenly with the sliced chile. Squeeze 1 lemon half evenly over the avocado halves.

In a separate bowl, toss the arugula with the olive oil and $1^1/_2$ tablespoons juice from the remaining lemon half. Sprinkle with salt.

Top each avocado half with the arugula salad and serve.

Miner's Lettuce, Fava Beans, English Peas, and Spring Garlic
with White Balsamic Vinaigrette

There are as many springtime things in this salad as possible. In Seattle, we have so much rain that when spring comes, it comes HARD—favas, nettles, peas, spring garlic, and a host of wild little greens that go perfectly together. Regular balsamic vinegar is too heavy; white balsamic still has the sweetness, but it's lighter and allows the flavors of the vegetables to really shine through. This recipe makes more vinaigrette than you'll need for the salad. Use the remaining dressing on other combinations of delicate spring vegetables and greens.

1$^1/_2$ pounds fava beans, shucked

1 cup English peas, shucked

2 stalks spring garlic, stem only
(reserve bulb for another use)

$^1/_2$ cup plus 2 tablespoons extra-virgin olive oil

Kosher salt

$^1/_4$ cup white balsamic vinegar

2 tablespoons water

1 fresh egg yolk

1 teaspoon Dijon mustard

$^1/_2$ cup canola oil

6 cups loosely packed miner's lettuce

Pecorino Toscano, for serving

Bring a large pot of water to a boil and prepare an ice-water bath. Blanch the favas for 1 to 2 minutes, to loosen skins, then shock in the ice-water bath. Slip off the skins. Repeat with the peas, blanching for 1 minute and then shocking in ice water. Set aside to drain thoroughly.

Thinly slice the stems of the garlic. Heat 2 tablespoons of the olive oil in a skillet over low heat and sauté the garlic with a pinch of salt—simply warming it through with the salt helps bring out the moisture—for 10 minutes.

Combine the vinegar, water, egg yolk, mustard, and a pinch of salt in the jar of a blender. Pulse to combine, then add the canola oil and $^1/_4$ cup of the olive oil in a slow, steady stream. Reserve.

Place the lettuce, fava beans, and peas in a bowl. Top with the garlic. Add enough vinaigrette to lightly coat the vegetables and greens and toss gently to combine. Divide among 4 plates and shave a few chards pecorino over the top of each, using a vegetable peeler to make large curls. Serve immediately.

Panzanella with Crispy Pig's Ear

I'm an ear man—if we're talking pig. Crispy pig's ears are gelatinous, cartilaginous, rich, chewy goodness that make an awfully lovely garnish for a fresh panzanella bursting with summer vegetables.

You'll want to allow about half an ear per person, which should amount to about a pound, depending on the pigs, of course. As with many of the best cuts of the pig, it takes a while to get ears into a perfect state for eating. You can boil them, but to get them perfectly tender and ready for frying, I like to poach them in oil first. You need to plan ahead—they take about six hours in a slow oven—but you could do that the day before, or even in the evening when it's cooler out, then finish them off the day you're going to serve them.

Note: When you fry pig's ears, use a covered fryer if you have one. If you don't, stand back, I mean way back, or better yet, go have a glass of wine in the other room while they cook. They pop and sputter like crazy. Yes, you'll have to clean the kitchen floor when you're done, but once you're chewing that ear, I promise you, you won't mind.

PIG'S EARS

3 pig's ears, halved

4 cloves garlic, smashed

6 sprigs thyme

Extra-virgin olive oil, for poaching and frying

PANZANELLA

1/2 baguette, cubed

7 tablespoons extra-virgin olive oil

Kosher salt and freshly ground pepper

4 ounces fresh beans, trimmed

8 oil-packed anchovy fillets, chopped

1 clove garlic, thinly sliced crosswise

1/2 pound ripe heirloom tomatoes, cut into large chunks

Juice of 1 lemon

1/4 red onion

Preheat the oven to 350°F.

To prepare the pig's ears, wash them well under cold running water. Put them in a deep-sided braising dish with the garlic and thyme and cover completely with olive oil. Cover with foil and poach for 5 to 6 hours, or until completely tender. You can strain the poaching oil through a fine-mesh sieve and keep for frying and sautéing.

Up to 2 hours before serving, bring 3 inches of oil to 350°F in a deep-fat fryer or Dutch oven. Remove the ears from the braising pan and cut each in half. Fry for 6 to 8 minutes, or until crispy all the way through. Set aside on a wire rack to drain.

(continued)

To make the panzanella, preheat the oven to 350°F. Bring a pot of water to a boil and prepare an ice-water bath.

Toss the bread cubes with 3 tablespoons of the olive oil and season with salt and pepper. Bake until slightly dry but still chewy in the center, about 15 minutes.

Place the anchovies and garlic in a large bowl with the remaining 4 tablespoons olive oil and a pinch of salt and pepper. Add the tomatoes, and lemon juice. Shave the onion on a mandoline and add to the mixture. Add the bread cubes and allow to sit for 10 to 15 minutes, stirring occasionally.

To serve, divide the panzanella among 6 shallow bowls. Garnish each bowl with half a fried ear.

Potato and Asparagus Salad with Home-Cured Bacon and Egg

This is my idea of bacon and eggs. Thick, homemade bacon adding a smoky, salty touch to gorgeous spring asparagus and tender new-crop potatoes, all crowned with a perfectly poached egg—it doesn't get much better than this. When you break into the soft yolk, it melts into the vegetables, forming a luxurious sauce. This recipe makes four hearty portions. If you would like to serve six smaller plates, keep the other quantities the same and simply increase the number of eggs.

Kosher salt and freshly cracked pepper

3/4 pound new or fingerling potatoes

1 bunch asparagus

1/4 cup extra-virgin olive oil, plus more for drizzling

2 stalks green garlic, thinly sliced on the diagonal

1/2 pound Home-Cured Bacon (page 146), diced

2 tablespoons chopped fresh parsley

1/2 lemon

4 fresh eggs, at room temperature

Bring a large pot of salted water to a boil over high heat and add the potatoes. Cook until just tender, 10 to 12 minutes, then transfer to a baking sheet to dry. When cool enough to handle, peel the potatoes and cut into thick slices. Season to taste with salt and pepper and place in a deep bowl.

Snap off the ends of the asparagus spears at their natural breaking point and cut into 1-inch lengths. Heat a sauté pan over medium-high heat and add 2 tablespoons of the olive oil. Add the asparagus and green garlic and sauté until the asparagus is tender and the garlic is soft, 3 to 4 minutes. Add to the bowl with the potatoes.

Wipe out the pan and add the bacon, cooking until the bacon crisps slightly and renders some of its fat. Remove with a slotted spoon and add to the bowl. Toss and season to taste with salt and plenty of freshly cracked pepper. Add the remaining 2 tablespoons olive oil and the parsley, then squeeze the lemon over all. Toss and divide among 4 plates.

Fill a wide pan, at least 3 inches deep, with enough water to cover the eggs and bring to a gentle simmer over low heat. Bubbles should lazily break the surface. Crack the eggs into small bowls or ramekins, then one by one gently slide the eggs into the water. Use a spoon or spatula to gently gather the whites around the yolks.

Cook for 2 to 3 minutes, depending on how firm you like your yolks. Remove the eggs, blotting each briefly on paper towels, then gently place on top of each salad. Drizzle with additional olive oil and serve immediately.

Thumbelina Carrots with Orange and Mint

Many recipes that pair carrots with orange call for cooking the carrots with orange juice. Here, I use strips of peel instead, so that you get just a hint of orange, keeping the flavors bright. In the restaurants, we use Thumbelina carrots, a cute, round variety with incredible sweetness. Don't go crazy chopping the mint—you don't want to turn it into paste. Just do a few quick strokes with the knife, toss with the carrots, and serve right away. You might want to caution your guests not to eat the orange peel.

1 pound Thumbelina carrots, peeled and trimmed

2 tablespoons extra-virgin olive oil

Kosher salt and freshly ground pepper

1 orange

1/2 cup fresh mint leaves

Depending on the size of the carrots, cut them in half or quarter them to maintain evenly sized pieces. Heat the olive oil in a sauté pan over medium-high heat and add the carrots. Toss until the carrots are well browned and caramelized. You want them to get good color without burning. Season with salt and pepper.

With a vegetable peeler, cut 4 large swaths of peel from the orange. Add to the carrots and toss for a minute more. Roughly chop the mint leaves and add to the pan. Toss and serve immediately.

Pheromone Salad (Shaved Porcini Salad)

I have to say that this is one of my all-time favorite salads, my variation of an Alice Waters recipe I came across years ago, and I've always loved the simplicity and the flavor. Shave the mushrooms immediately prior to serving, so that they release their aromas. It's so intoxicating that you'd think they were pheromones. This salad is actually pretty sexy.

$^{1}/_{2}$ pound button porcini mushrooms, shaved with a mandoline

$^{1}/_{2}$ cup best-quality olive oil

1 teaspoon fresh lemon juice

Kosher salt and freshly cracked pepper

Parmigiano-Reggiano, for serving

You need to make each salad individually so the gentle shavings don't get bruised or broken. With this few ingredients, everything must be perfect, so take your time and allow yourself to feel the art of creating each plate.

Set out 4 dinner plates. Gently divide the porcini slices among the plates, spreading them out on the plates almost like a carpaccio. Drizzle the olive oil over the top and sprinkle with lemon juice. Sprinkle with salt, and crack pepper to taste over each salad. Using a vegetable peeler, shave Parmigiano-Reggiano over the top of each and serve.

Swiss Chard with Pine Nuts and Golden Raisins

Swiss chard, with fleshy stems that offer nice texture, has a milder flavor than other greens such as rapini or mustard. I highlight its sweetness with golden raisins and white wine, then add pine nuts for richness and some crunch. Be sure to dry the chard carefully before sautéing, because it gives off a lot of liquid.

1/2 cup golden raisins

1/4 cup white wine

1/4 cup pine nuts

2 bunches Swiss chard

2 tablespoons extra-virgin olive oil

2 cloves garlic, thinly sliced

Kosher salt and freshly ground pepper

Preheat the oven to 350°F.

Put the raisins and wine in a small saucepan and bring just to a boil. Remove from the heat and set aside for the raisins to macerate while you prepare the rest of the dish.

Spread the pine nuts out on a baking sheet. Toast in the oven just until lightly browned, about 10 minutes. Watch the nuts carefully. They have a high fat content and will color quickly. Transfer to a plate to cool.

Separate the chard into leaves, trimming back the thick stems but leaving the leaves whole. Swish in cool water, then carefully pat or spin dry.

Heat the oil in a sauté pan over medium heat and add the garlic. Sauté for about 30 seconds, then add the chard. Stir to coat the leaves in oil. Add the raisins and wine. Cook until the chard is totally wilted and the wine has mostly evaporated, 5 to 7 minutes. Season with salt and pepper to taste and serve.

Beasties of the Land . . .

My perfect cut of meat, red meat, is a two-pound rib-eye. I love a big, roasted chunk that you bring to the table and let people tear into like they were wild beasts themselves. In fact, there's something about a hunk of meat on the bone that brings out the animal in most of us. If I have my druthers, I'll always cook meat on the bone. You get better flavor, you get better yield, and it's easier to prepare. The sad thing about my perfect meat is that it's hard to do in restaurants; I guess people don't want other diners to see their Henry VIII side. The good news is that it's nice to be able to make dishes like that rib-eye at home and share them with the people you like to hang around with the most. Someone gets to take charge of the table (people love it when someone takes control), carving off strips and slices for everyone to enjoy. It's carnal— literally—it's fun, and it's good.

In fact, I like the big-meat option so much I've included five special recipes in this section that I like to categorize as "party meats." Unlike venison or duck or sweetbreads—meats so rich I would only do small portions as part of a multicourse meal—these are dishes meant to be served family-style on big platters. From a whole lamb shoulder served with crespelle as Italian "tacos" to a rich pot of silky tripe, this is food meant to be shared, food meant for adventure. So go ahead, rub a whole goat leg with Syrian spices and roast it off. Braise a whole rabbit and invite your friends to eat right out of the pot. That's a dinner party I want to attend.

Overall, I like meat with deep flavor, and I'll gladly trade a buttery texture for some richness and chew. That is why, though there are plenty of chicken dishes that I like, nary a chicken appears in the pages that follow. There are thousands of other cookbooks where you can get those recipes if you want them. In terms of our feathered friends, I've chosen to concentrate instead on duck and diminutive birds, such as quail and squab, that have amazing flavor. I like to roast the latter two whole; it's so nice to gnaw the little bones and have a whole bird all to yourself.

Braised Pork Jowls with the Maligned Mélange

The much-maligned mélange gets its name from the undeserved yet pervasive bad reps held by each of the three principal ingredients in this delectable side: turnips, Brussels sprouts, and chestnuts. But I guarantee you'll find that baby turnips are sweet and juicy and bear no resemblance to the bitter root vegetable you think you know. Gently sautéing wedges of fresh Brussels sprouts renders them crisp-tender and nutty, while browning chestnuts in a cast-iron pan makes removing their skins a snap, giving you unfettered access to the earthiness inside.

Pork jowls, as the name implies, are pig cheeks. When cured, jowls become *guanciale*; braised, they offer amazing versatility and can then be sautéed, grilled, or added to soups. Like pork belly, jowls have tons of flavor and are very rich. I find that braising helps tame them a bit and makes the cut a little less intense. You'll probably need to special order this cut from your butcher, but it's worth it. You'll need to start this recipe one day ahead.

4 of the smallest pork jowls you can find

2 carrots, peeled and roughly chopped

3 stalks celery, roughly chopped

1 head garlic, unpeeled, sliced in half horizontally

1 onion, chopped

2 fresh bay leaves

1 teaspoon peppercorns

1/2 pound fresh chestnuts

1/2 pound Brussels sprouts

1/2 pound small turnips (about 2 bunches)

2 tablespoons unsalted butter

Kosher salt and freshly cracked black pepper

2 tablespoons extra-virgin olive oil

1 teaspoon chopped fresh thyme leaves

Preheat the oven to 350°F.

Place the meat, carrots, celery, garlic, onion, bay leaves, and peppercorns in a high-sided ovenproof pan with enough room for the jowls to move around and add water to cover by 1 inch. Cover the pan with foil or a tight-fitting lid and braise for 3 1/2 to 4 hours, or until a paring knife slides through the meat easily.

Remove the jowls from the liquid, place in a shallow pan, and cover with a plate. Discard the liquid and vegetables. Put a couple of cans or a cast-iron pot on top of the plate to press the jowls and refrigerate overnight.

Increase the oven temperature to 375°F.

Prepare the chestnuts by cutting an X in the pointed end of each with a sharp knife. Heat a cast-iron skillet as hot as you can get it and place the chestnuts inside in a single layer. Brown for about 1 minute on the first side. Using tongs, flip the chestnuts and brown for 1 to $1^1/_2$ minutes longer. The color will darken and become spotted with black. Remove the pan from the heat and let cool. When the chestnuts are completely cool, the shells should pop off easily. Quarter the chestnuts and set aside.

Remove any tough outer leaves from the Brussels sprouts by snapping them off at the base. Trim the base and quarter each sprout. Trim the stalks of the turnips and peel. Quarter lengthwise.

Heat the butter in a sauté pan over medium-high heat. Add the turnips and Brussels sprouts and stir to coat in butter. Cook until golden brown and charred in places, stirring frequently, 5 to 6 minutes total, adding the chestnuts half-way through the cooking time.

While the vegetables are cooking, season the jowls liberally on both sides with kosher salt and plenty of cracked black pepper. Heat the olive oil in an ovenproof sauté pan over high heat and sear the jowls for 5 minutes with the fatty side down. Pop the pan in the oven and roast for an additional 5 minutes, or until crispy, golden, and heated through.

When the vegetables are done, season with salt and pepper and toss with the thyme. Serve with the jowls.

Home-Cured Bacon

You must believe me when I tell you that making sweet, smoky, succulent bacon with your own two hands is an undertaking you will never regret. It adds something indescribable to dishes like Potato and Asparagus Salad with Home-Cured Bacon and Egg (page 137), and tastes pretty amazing alongside a fried egg. In the restaurants, we cure our own and use it in everything from pastas to panzanella to lentils.

Aleppo is a medium-spicy, fruity red pepper that comes from Syria. It has a nice complexity and heat that vanishes almost the minute you notice it's there. You can find it in Middle Eastern groceries and on the Internet. For this recipe, you'll need four days, a smoker, and wood chips, preferably hickory.

1 fresh pork belly, skin removed, 7 to 9 pounds

2 to 3 tablespoons ground Aleppo pepper, to taste

3 pounds kosher salt

1 teaspoon curing salt

1 pound granulated sugar

1 pound brown sugar

Rub the pork belly top and bottom with the Aleppo pepper. Combine the kosher salt, curing salt, granulated sugar, and brown sugar in a large, nonreactive container and bury the belly completely in the mixture. Cover and refrigerate for 2 days.

Remove the belly from the refrigerator and discard the cure. Rinse the remaining cure off the meat and pat it dry. Set the belly on a baking sheet and loosely cover. Allow to sit in the refrigerator another 2 days. On the second day, set the hickory chips in water to soak overnight.

Using a conventional smoker, smoke the belly until the internal temperature reaches 145°F. Once the belly is smoked and cooled, cut into 4 sections. Wrap the sections well in plastic wrap and foil and store in the freezer until needed, up to 3 months.

Lamb Chops with Finger Favas

This is your grown-up chance to play with your food! Frenched lamb chops, also known as lamb lollipops, just beg to be picked up and gnawed on because the clean bones make lovely handles. Even the veg gets in on the interactive eating, with tender spring favas sautéed in their skins. Besides being fun finger food, there's an added perk to cooking them this way: because they're not blanched, the favas stay extra-sweet and firm. Just pick them up one by one and pop them into your mouth, like edamame served in Japanese restaurants. Don't bother setting forks or knives at the table, but I recommend providing plenty of napkins.

8 lamb chops

Kosher salt and freshly ground pepper

2 tablespoons chopped fresh parsley

2 tablespoons chopped fresh mint

2 cloves garlic, sliced

Extra-virgin olive oil, for drizzling

Finger Favas, for accompaniment (recipe follows)

You can ask your butcher to French the lamb chops for you, or you can do it yourself. If you are beginning with a whole rack, first run your knife horizontally across the rack 2 to $2^1/_2$ inches from the ends of the bones where the chop broadens. Flip the rack over and repeat on the other side, making the cuts parallel to one another. Next, cut out the meat connecting the bones, cutting along each bone down to the horizontal cuts you have already made. Remove these fingers of meat and fat. Discard. Cut through the rack to separate it into evenly sized chops. Tilt one chop vertically, holding the bone end in one hand with the meat resting on your cutting board. Take a sharp knife and place the blade against the bone. Scrape along the bone in short, smooth movements, as if you were peeling a carrot, cleaning the bone and pushing the meat toward the cutting board to form a meat "lollipop" with a bone handle. Once the long portion of the bone is cleaned and scraped, trim off any remaining meat and fat at the base of the bone. Repeat with the remaining chops.

Pat the chops dry and season both sides with salt and pepper. Place the chops in a baking dish just big enough to hold them. Sprinkle with the parsley, mint, and sliced garlic and drizzle olive oil generously over the top. Allow the chops to marinate for at least 2 hours.

When ready to serve, preheat a grill to high or prepare a hot fire. Grill the chops until seared, about 2 minutes per side. Set aside to rest while you prepare the fava beans.

FINGER FAVAS

2 tablespoons unsalted butter

2 tablespoons extra-virgin olive oil

2 cloves garlic, sliced

Kosher salt

2 cups fava beans, shelled, with the skins on

Heat the butter and olive oil in a sauté pan over medium heat. Add the garlic and a pinch of salt and stir to coat. Add the favas. Sauté for 5 minutes, or until the fava beans are just tender. Serve with the grilled lamb chops.

Venison Loin with Cipollini Agrodolce

After a rugged weekend of deer hunting, this is the dish I celebrate with . . . okay, not really. I buy farmed venison, just as you will. The nice thing, other than not having to don your camo and risk getting ticks, is that farmed venison is less intense than wild deer meat, with a rich, sophisticated flavor that is perfectly accented with a simple *agrodolce*. Forget about beef tenderloin and serve this instead—I promise the luscious texture and wild essence will win you over. As with tenderloin, though, make sure you serve the venison rare.

1 pound cipollini onions

2 cups red wine

1/4 cup red wine vinegar

3 tablespoons sugar

Kosher salt and freshly ground pepper

2 tablespoons extra-virgin olive oil

4 (4-ounce) portions venison loin
(also called medallions)

Peel the onions and trim the tops, keeping the root end intact. Combine the onions, wine, vinegar, and sugar in a medium saucepan over medium-high heat, bring to a boil and add a pinch of salt. Decrease the heat to maintain a brisk simmer and cook until the onions are tender and the liquid has reduced to a syrup, about 15 minutes. Remember that the *agrodolce* will continue to thicken as it cools.

Heat the olive oil in 1 large or 2 medium sauté pans over high heat. Season the loin pieces with salt and pepper and sear, no more than 2 minutes per side. Transfer to a plate and let rest for 10 minutes or so.

Cut each loin in half horizontally. Lean the halves against each other at opposing angles. Spoon the *agrodolce* next to the meats and drizzle some over the top. Serve immediately.

Veal Sweetbreads with Parsley, Capers, and Lemon

This riff on veal piccata is not a complicated dish, but it does have a few steps to it and requires some planning to allow the sweetbreads time to soak overnight. Poaching the sweetbreads in milk and aromatics before sautéing them ensures they'll turn out sweet and meltingly tender. I prefer veal sweetbreads, though you can use lamb. Either one is usually sold in one-pound packs, with two large lobes per pack. If you don't see them out on display—they're usually not—ask the butcher if there are any in back, and make sure they are impeccably fresh. The delicate richness of the dish means that nothing more than boiled potatoes are needed as an accompaniment.

2 pounds veal sweetbreads

1 large carrot, peeled and chopped

1 small onion, peeled and halved

2 stalks celery, cut in half horizontally

1 head garlic, halved horizontally

About 1/2 gallon milk

2 lemons

Kosher salt and freshly ground pepper

Flour, for coating

1/2 cup extra-virgin olive oil, plus more for drizzling

2 tablespoons unsalted butter

2 tablespoons salt-packed capers, rinsed

1 tablespoon chopped fresh parsley

The night before you plan to serve the sweetbreads, set them to soak in a bowl of water in the refrigerator. You'll want to change the water a few times to make sure you remove any traces of blood or impurities. When ready to cook, drain and rinse.

Put the sweetbreads in a large saucepan along with the carrot, onion, celery, and garlic. Cover with milk by 1 inch, and bring to a boil over medium-high heat. Reduce the heat and simmer for 10 to 12 minutes, or until just cooked through.

Remove the sweetbreads and discard the milk and vegetables. Place on a plate, then top with another plate. Add a weight to the top plate—2 heavy cans or a cast-iron pan would do—and put in the fridge until they are completely cool, at least 2 hours.

While the sweetbreads are cooling, cut a slice off both ends of one of the lemons. Standing the lemon on end, slice strips from top to bottom, removing all the peel and pith. Repeat until there is no peel left. Then slice between the membranes to release the individual segments. Dice the segments and reserve. Juice the second lemon and reserve.

When the sweetbreads are cool, pat them dry. Divide them gently into individual lobes—there should be 1 large lobe per person. (Save scraps for stuffing or for a chef's treat.) Season with salt and pepper and coat each lightly with flour.

Divide the olive oil between 2 sauté pans and heat over medium-high heat. When the oil is hot, carefully add the sweetbreads to the oil and brown all over, about 2 minutes per side.

Transfer to a plate and drain the oil. Wipe out the pans, place over medium heat, and return the sweetbreads to the pans. Divide the butter, diced lemon, capers, and lemon juice between the pans. Swirl the sauce and use a spoon to coat the sweetbreads. Place the sweetbreads on 4 plates, drizzle with olive oil, sprinkle with parsley, and serve.

Seared Duck Breast with Sugared Figs and Arugula

For those of you who crave the ubiquitous duck breast all dressed up for company, I offer you my version, the little ducky paired with sweet-and-sour roasted figs and given a little edge from the arugula. I won't lie—it's good. However, in exchange for my providing a traditional duck breast recipe, you must promise me that you will try either Party Tripe on Soft Polenta (page 159) or maybe Geoduck Crudo with Fennel and Radish (page 24). Do what scares you.

12 Kadota or Mission figs

6 tablespoons extra-virgin olive oil

Rock or turbinado sugar, for sprinkling

1 teaspoon Chianti vinegar

4 (5- or 6-ounce) duck breasts, skin on

1 bunch arugula

1 teaspoon fresh lemon juice

Kosher salt and freshly ground pepper

Preheat the oven to 400°F.

Wipe the figs clean, remove the stems, then halve them lengthwise. Place the figs, cut-side up, on a wire rack set on a foil-lined baking sheet. Drizzle the figs with 2 tablespoons of the olive oil, then sprinkle with the sugar. Roast in the oven for about 15 minutes, or until soft. Drizzle with the vinegar as soon as they come out of the oven. Decrease the oven temperature to 375°F.

Film the bottom of a large, ovenproof sauté pan with 2 tablespoons olive oil and heat over medium-low heat. Add the duck breasts, skin-side down, and cook for 8 to 10 minutes, or until most of the fat renders and the skin crisps. As the breasts sear, spoon off the excess fat as it pools in the pan. When the fat has rendered, transfer the breasts to a plate and pour off all the accumulated fat. Return the breasts, skin-side up, to the pan and transfer the pan to the oven. Roast for no more than 2 to 3 minutes, then remove the breasts from the pan and allow to rest while you make and dress the salad.

Pick off the smallest and most tender arugula leaves and wash well. Pat dry. Toss with the remaining 2 tablespoons olive oil and the lemon juice; season with salt and pepper.

Lay 3 figs out on each of 4 plates. Slice each duck breast on the diagonal and fan out over the figs, then nestle the arugula salad next to it.

Braised Veal Cheeks with Grilled Ramps and Porcini

Veal cheeks make the most delicate braise. Using a combination of water and wine for the braising liquid allows the sweet, subtle taste of the veal to really shine through. As a side, you need nothing more than the spring's first ramps and some gorgeous porcini, kissed by the grill.

Some years, it just so happens that the ramp season runs long, or perhaps the porcini season starts early, or both. When the two magically coincide, some amazing things happen. Using foil as insulation for the delicate ramp tops gives the vegetables a simple char on the grill. The veal needs time to become fork-tender, a few hours in all, so plan accordingly.

2 pounds trimmed veal cheeks, 8 pieces in all (trimmed of any excess fat and sinew)

Kosher salt and freshly ground pepper

1/4 cup extra-virgin olive oil

2 carrots, peeled and roughly chopped

4 cloves garlic, smashed

1 onion, chopped

2 cups white wine

2 cups water

2 fresh bay leaves

Grilled Ramps and Porcini, for accompaniment (recipe follows)

Preheat the oven to 350°F.

Season the cheeks liberally with salt and pepper on both sides. Using 2 sauté pans to avoid crowding, heat 2 tablespoons olive oil in each pan over high heat. Sear the veal cheeks for 2 to 3 minutes per side, or until caramelized.

Transfer to a braising dish. Divide the carrots, garlic, and onion between the pans and sauté just until they get a hint of color, 2 to 3 minutes. Deglaze the pans with the wine and empty the vegetables and the wine into the braising dish with the meat. Add the water and bay leaves. Cover the dish with foil or a heavy, tight-fitting lid and braise for 2 1/2 to 3 hours, or until meltingly tender.

Transfer the veal cheeks to a plate and strain the liquid through a fine-mesh sieve into a clean pan. Bring to a boil, then reduce to a brisk simmer. Reduce the braising liquid until it becomes a syrupy glaze and measures 1/2 cup. Add the veal cheeks to the pan and warm through in the liquid. Place 2 cheeks on each of 4 plates and spoon the remaining glaze over the top. Serve with the Grilled Ramps and Porcini.

GRILLED RAMPS AND PORCINI

20 to 24 ramps, rinsed and trimmed

4 porcini mushrooms, smaller than a tennis ball, bigger than a golf ball, wiped clean and halved lengthwise

Extra-virgin olive oil, for grilling and drizzling

Kosher salt and freshly cracked pepper

Preheat the grill on high or light a hot charcoal fire. Rub the ramps and mushrooms with olive oil and season with salt and pepper. Lay a piece of foil down on half of the grill. Place the ramps on the grill with the tops resting on top of the foil, the bulbs on the grate. Place the mushrooms, cut-side down, directly on the grill. Grill, turning frequently, until tender and browned in spots. Drizzle with olive oil and serve with the veal cheeks.

Skillet-Roasted Rabbit with Pancetta-Basted Fingerlings

SERVES 4

This is a very rustic dish, the meat and potatoes redolent with rosemary and garlic and bathed in butter and pork fat. But as rich as all of that sounds, the best part might be the front legs that end up crispy and delicious; as you gnaw the bones, you'll be reminded more than a little of fried chicken, and that's never a bad thing. I portion out the rabbit so that the darker pieces get a little more cooking and the loin receives nothing more than a quick sear. As with Braised Rabbit Paws with Radiatore (page 89), make sure you ask the butcher for the smaller and more tender fryers, not roasters.

3 tablespoons unsalted butter

1 pound fingerling potatoes, halved lengthwise

8 ounces pancetta, diced

2 sprigs rosemary

3 fat cloves garlic, smashed

2 fryer rabbits

Kosher salt and freshly ground pepper

3 tablespoons extra-virgin olive oil

2 tablespoons chopped fresh parsley

Preheat the oven to 400°F.

In an ovenproof sauté pan, heat the butter over medium-high heat. Add the potatoes, cut-side down, and cook for about 5 minutes, or until they begin to brown. Add the pancetta, rosemary, and garlic and toss to combine. Place the pan in the oven and roast until the potatoes are tender and the pancetta is crisp, 10 to 12 minutes. Remove from the oven, discard the rosemary, and place the potatoes, garlic, and pancetta on paper towels to drain the excess fat. Reserve.

To prepare the rabbits, using a sharp knife, begin by removing the front legs at the joint and set aside. Next, slice off the loins, or the strips of meat that run along the backbone of each rabbit. Slice each loin into rough 1-inch chunks and reserve. Finally, debone the back legs, cutting the meat off the bone in pieces about the same size as the loin slices. Keep the leg meat separate from the pieces of loin. Season all the rabbit pieces with salt and pepper.

In a cast-iron skillet, heat the olive oil over medium heat. Add the front legs and back leg pieces and brown very well, turning frequently, 4 to 5 minutes. When the rabbit legs are mahogany, add the loin pieces and sear on both sides. Remove immediately and place on the plate with the potatoes, allowing the residual heat to finish cooking the meat. When ready to serve, return the rabbit meat to the skillet along with the potatoes, pancetta, and garlic. Cook until the potatoes are heated through. Add the parsley, toss, and serve from the pan.

Roast Quail Stuffed with Pancetta, Lacinato Kale, and Sage

When you buy your quail, try to get the biggest ones you can find, and make sure they're semi-boneless, meaning only the drumsticks and wings are left intact for the shape of the finished bird. When you're working with a bird this tiny, having someone else bone it is helpful. If you have mad knife skills, go for it. Using foil strips like huge twist ties helps set the shape of the quail as they cook, resulting in a pleasingly plump little package. Soft Polenta (page 66) and braised greens are the perfect accompaniments.

4 tablespoons extra-virgin olive oil, plus more if needed

4 ounces pancetta, diced

1 large carrot, peeled and diced

2 stalks celery, diced

3 cloves garlic, sliced

1 bunch Lacinato kale, washed, stemmed, and torn into pieces

1 cup chicken stock

3 cups 1/2-inch cubes stale bread

Kosher salt and freshly ground pepper

6 leaves sage, roughly chopped

4 semi-boneless quail

4 teaspoons unsalted butter

Preheat the oven to 350°F.

Warm 2 tablespoons of the olive oil in a sauté pan over medium heat and add the pancetta. Cook until some of the fat renders, about 4 minutes. Add the carrot, celery, and garlic and sauté until tender but not colored, 3 to 4 minutes. Add the kale and sauté until just wilted, about 1 minute. Add the chicken stock and cook down until the liquid nearly evaporates and the mixture is thick, 3 to 4 minutes. Place the mixture in a large bowl with the bread cubes and toss to mix. Season to taste with salt and pepper. Add the sage and additional olive oil if necessary to moisten. Allow the mixture to cool before stuffing the birds.

Season each quail on both sides with salt and pepper. Pack the quail as tightly as possible, using about 1 cup of stuffing per bird. Tuck the wings under the bird behind the back. Bend one drumstick across the cavity opening, keeping the stuffing in place. Secure by tucking the tip under the skin. Cross the other drumstick over it so that the quail looks like it's doing yoga.

Tear off about 5 inches of foil. Fold the long end up about 1 inch, crease, then keep folding and creasing until you have a reinforced band 1 inch tall and as long as your box of foil. Wrap the band around the quail to secure, twisting the ends. Trim off extra foil with scissors. Make 3 more bands the same way and repeat with the remaining birds.

Divide the remaining 2 tablespoons olive oil between two 10-inch ovenproof sauté pans, and warm over high heat. Brown the quail on each side, about 1 minute each, including the foil-wrapped sides. Once you turn the quail to brown the top, top each with 1 teaspoon butter and put the pans in the oven. After 5 minutes, turn each quail so that the top of the bird is up. Roast for 5 minutes longer, or until a metal skewer inserted into the middle of the stuffing feels warm against your lip.

Once the quail are done, transfer to a board and remove the foil. Return to the pan to crisp the skin and brown the sides that were under the foil strips. Serve.

Pan-Roasted Squab with Spring Garlic Compote

Save this recipe for late February, when spring garlic first appears in markets. For this dish, it's best to use larger heads, planning on one large or two small heads per serving.

Piecing out the squab makes for much easier eating and allows you to cook the different parts perfectly, with the added bonus that the wings and body add incredible depth and flavor to the sauce. If you think your knife skills aren't up to par, you can ask your butcher to do it for you, but be sure to reserve all the pieces. If your guests are big eaters, you might want to double the recipe to allow for one squab per person and serve as an entrée. Lentils would make a nice side.

2 squab

1/4 cup plus 2 tablespoons extra-virgin olive oil

2 carrots, peeled and chopped

1 small onion, peeled and chopped

3 cloves garlic, halved

3 cups red wine

2 cups chicken stock

8 small or 4 large bulbs spring garlic

2 tablespoons honey

Kosher salt and freshly ground pepper

Remove the breasts, thighs, and drumsticks from the squab and reserve. Using a large chef's knife, chop the bodies and wings into 3 or 4 pieces. Heat 2 tablespoons of the olive oil in a large saucepan over high heat. Add the squab bones and parts and sauté until well browned. Add the carrots, onion, and garlic cloves. Cook until softened and lightly colored, 6 to 8 minutes in all, then add 2 cups of the wine. Continue to cook until reduced by three-quarters, 6 to 8 minutes, then add the chicken stock. Bring to a boil, reduce the heat, and simmer for 1 hour. Strain the mixture through a fine-mesh sieve over a bowl, pressing on the solids to extract all the liquid. You should end up with about 2 cups liquid. Discard the solids. Put the liquid in a clean saucepan and reduce until syrupy, or 1/4 cup total; the timing will vary depending on your stove and pan, but will be about 15 minutes.

To make the compote, cut the spring garlic bulbs from the stems, then slice crosswise 1/8 inch thick. Film a sauté pan with 2 tablespoons of the olive oil and heat over high heat. Fry the garlic until crisp and lightly browned, 1 to 2 minutes. Pour off the oil. Add the remaining 1 cup wine to the pan and cook over medium heat until reduced to about 2 tablespoons, about 10 minutes. Add the honey and cook until the mixture is thickened and coats the back of a spoon, 4 to 5 minutes. Reserve at room temperature.

In a large sauté pan over high heat, heat the remaining 2 tablespoons olive oil on high heat and fry the squab breasts, thighs, and drumsticks skin-side down first, putting a light weight on the breasts or pressing with a spatula, for about 3 minutes. Turn the pieces and cook for 2 minutes longer, then turn once more to crisp the skin and finish cooking. Breasts should be served medium-rare, while thighs and drumsticks are cooked through. Allow to rest for 5 to 10 minutes before serving.

When ready to serve, reheat the sauce and season with salt and pepper. Divide the compote among 4 plates and place the squab pieces on top. Spoon the sauce around the squab and serve.

Party Tripe on Soft Polenta

SERVES 8

The next time you feel like throwing a raging party for all your tripe-loving friends, this is the dish for you! If you're making a face while reading this allow me to offer a cliché: don't knock it 'til you've tried it. Yes, even the best honeycomb tripe could be described as mild with an edge of musk. But all that means is that it needs a good, savory vehicle to deliver that fabulous texture straight to your mouth. Here, tomato sauce enhances the flavor, while beans provide a creamy textural counterpoint. I add mint, too, to give it some zing. This is a truly comforting dish that would be especially welcome on a cold fall or winter evening.

1 pound honeycomb tripe, rinsed well

1 onion, peeled and halved

1 head garlic, halved horizontally

2 tablespoons vinegar

Kosher salt and freshly ground pepper

2 tablespoons extra-virgin olive oil

4 cloves garlic, thinly sliced

3 cups Basic Tomato Sauce (page 216)

1 cup Controne Beans (page 162) with
1 cup cooking liquid

2 sprigs mint, leaves picked and roughly chopped

1 recipe Soft Polenta (page 66)

Put the tripe in a large pot and cover with 2 inches of water. Add the onion, garlic head, vinegar, and a good pinch of salt. Weight the tripe down with either a pot lid or a plate and bring to a brisk simmer. Cook for 1 to 1^1/$_2$ hours, or until the tripe is completely tender. Drain the tripe, discard the vegetables and liquid, and slice the tripe into thick ribbons.

Heat the olive oil in a sauté pan over medium heat and add the sliced garlic. Sauté for 2 to 3 minutes, until soft, then add the tripe and a pinch of salt and a grind or two of pepper. Sauté for 2 to 3 minutes longer, then add the tomato sauce and bean cooking liquid. Simmer for 5 minutes, then add the beans. Cook until the beans are heated through, about 2 minutes more. Add the mint and stir to combine.

For each diner, spoon a puddle of polenta into the bottom of a shallow bowl. Ladle a generous cup of the stew over the top and serve.

PARTY MEATS

Once you set out an array of dishes on a table it feels festive. That said, there's nothing like a big pot of spicy tripe, a roasted animal leg, or a tender chunk of meat that guests go after like wolves to add a certain party atmosphere to any gathering—family or friends. Think big, think bold, think party meats!

Beasties of the Land . . . 159

Zatar-Rubbed Leg of Goat with Fresh Chickpeas, Spring Onion, and Sorrel

In this pure celebration of spring, Middle Eastern spices add warmth and depth to tender goat, while the season's first tender offerings—fresh chickpeas, slender spring onions, tart sorrel—make a fabulous accompaniment. Letting the sautéed vegetables cool before adding the sorrel allows it to keep its vibrant color, and it also makes this relaxed, do-ahead party food. Prepare the side while the goat rests and be prepared to covet the leftovers.

Fresh chickpeas look like abbreviated little fava beans in the pod, and, like favas, they require a two-step shelling process to get to the little green gems inside. If you can find them, it's worth every minute of preparation. Fresh chickpeas are sweet and tender, with only a hint of the nuttiness that marks their flavor when dried. The spices can be found in Middle Eastern markets or online.

GOAT

2 teaspoons ground sumac

2 teaspoons ground coriander

2 teaspoons ground fennel seed

2 teaspoons ground Aleppo pepper

1 whole leg of goat, bone in (about $4^1/_2$ pounds)

CHICKPEAS

Kosher salt

1 pound fresh chickpeas, in the shell

4 spring onions

10 sprigs sorrel, washed well

2 tablespoons extra-virgin olive oil

Preheat the oven to 375°F.

To prepare the goat, combine the sumac, coriander, fennel, and Aleppo in a small bowl and rub into the goat leg, being sure to cover the entire surface of the meat with the spice rub. Roast the goat until the internal temperature reaches 130°F on a meat thermometer, about 1 hour. Remove the goat from the oven and allow to rest for at least 30 minutes before carving.

To make the chickpeas, bring a pot of salted water to a rapid boil and prepare an ice-water bath.

Remove the chickpeas from their outer shells. Add the chickpeas to the boiling water and blanch for 5 to 6 minutes, or until just tender and the outer skin is loose. Transfer immediately to the ice bath to cool. Drain. Carefully rub off their skins, trying to keep the chickpeas whole as you do. You should end up with a generous cup of chickpeas.

Peel and trim the onions, then cut crosswise into $^1/_4$-inch slices. Roughly chop the sorrel.

Heat the olive oil in a sauté pan over medium heat. Add the onions and cook gently over medium-low heat until tender, 8 to 10 minutes. Season with salt, then fold in the chickpeas and remove from the heat. Transfer the mixture to a bowl to cool before adding the sorrel. Check the seasoning. This dish is best served at room temperature.

Grilled T-Bone with Garlic, Lemon, and Controne Beans

A 3-pound T-bone makes a pretty fantastic, nearly Flintstonian presentation when you bring it to the table, marked from the grill. If you can, use your charcoal grill for this one—you've just spent a tidy sum on this gorgeous hunk of meat, why not give it the best flavor? Think of this as slow roasting—you're not cooking a hamburger here. A 3-pound steak gives you about 2 pounds of meat, 1/2 pound per person if you're feeding four. That's a good bit of steak, but somehow I don't think you'll have leftovers.

The creamy Controne bean is known as the "no-soak" bean because it lacks a hard skin. You could also use marrow or cannellini, both of which will require soaking, but try seeking out Controne beans in Italian markets.

1 (3-pound) T-bone steak

Kosher salt and freshly cracked pepper

2 tablespoons extra-virgin olive oil, plus more for grilling

2 cloves garlic, halved crosswise

1/4 lemon

Controne Beans, for accompaniment (recipe follows)

Trim the steak if necessary, leaving a good layer of fat. Season the meat very generously with salt and cracked pepper on both sides. Allow to sit for about 30 minutes on the counter. This gives the seasoning a chance to penetrate the meat and the steak time to come to room temperature.

Fire up your charcoal grill and wait until the coals are covered with a layer of ash. Brush the steak lightly with oil; don't use too much or you'll invite flames. Put the steak on the grill. If flare-ups occur, move the steak to a different part of the grill. Grill for 7 to 8 minutes on the first side, then turn the steak. Grill for 10 minutes on the second side.

Finish on the bone, balancing the steak on end to sear the meat and seal the edge.

Transfer the steak to a platter. Rub each side well with the cut side of a garlic clove, allowing the garlic to melt into the meat. Allow the meat to rest for at least 20 minutes and up to 30. When ready to carve, drizzle the olive oil over the meat and add a squeeze of lemon. Serve with the beans.

CONTRONE BEANS

1 cup Controne beans

1 head garlic, halved horizontally

1 large carrot, peeled and halved

2 stalks celery

1 thick slice lemon

1 clove garlic, smashed

1/4 cup extra-virgin olive oil

Kosher salt

Put the beans, garlic head, carrot, and celery in a large pot over high heat and cover with 2 inches of water. Bring to a boil, then lower the heat and simmer for 45 minutes to 1 hour, or until tender. Remove the vegetables and strain the beans, then put into a serving bowl. While the beans are still warm, add the lemon slice, garlic clove, olive oil, and salt to taste. The beans will absorb the flavors and seasoning as they cool; they will be ready to serve after 10 minutes, but are equally good served at room temperature.

Note: To prepare the beans ahead of time, cook until tender, then cool in their cooking liquid in the refrigerator. Reheat in the liquid, then strain and proceed with the recipe.

Italian "Tacos"

When I roast a lamb shoulder, I like to set a big hunk of meat in the middle of the table, letting everyone tear off a chunk of it and eat it like a group of happy Neanderthals. Crespelle are basically Italian crepes, and here they are used like tortillas, providing a delicious wrapper for hunks of lamb and creating what is basically an Italian taco. You need to use a 10-inch skillet to make the right size crespelle, and if you have a nonstick one this recipe will be foolproof. If you don't, brush or wipe the pan between crespelle with olive oil and you shouldn't have any problems. It's okay to make the crespelle ahead of time and leave them stacked and wrapped in a cloth.

1 tablespoon black peppercorns

1 tablespoon fennel seed

2 tablespoons dried Sicilian oregano

2 tablespoons chile flakes

1 bone-in lamb shoulder (about 10 pounds)

3 tablespoons Kosher salt

CRESPELLE

4 fresh eggs

2 cups all-purpose flour

2 cups 2 percent milk

1 teaspoon Kosher salt

$2^{1}/_{2}$ tablespoons unsalted butter, melted

Extra-virgin olive oil, for cooking

1 small red onion, minced

Preheat the oven to 300°F.

To prepare the lamb, place the peppercorns, fennel seed, oregano, and chile flakes in a spice grinder and process to a powder. Rub the lamb all over with the spice rub and salt and place on a baking sheet. Roast until the internal temperature reaches 145°F. Remove from the oven and allow to rest for at least 30 minutes before serving.

To make the crespelle, put the eggs, flour, milk, salt, and butter in a blender and process until smooth. Pour into a bowl and allow to rest at room temperature for 1 hour.

Lightly brush a 10-inch skillet with olive oil, wiping out the excess with a paper towel, and set over medium heat. Using a measuring cup, pour $^1/_4$ cup batter into the prepared skillet, tilting the pan to distribute the batter evenly. Cook until the underside is spotted with brown and the crespelle is set. Use the tip of a metal offset spatula to flip the crespelle. Immediately slide the crespelle out onto a plate lined with a kitchen towel. Repeat the process with the remaining batter.

To serve, allow your guests to pull meat off the roast and place on the crespelle. Top with minced red onion, wrap, and eat.

. . . and Sea

For a moment, set aside your preconceptions about the Pacific Northwest and salmon.
We have salmon, but we have so much more—fantastic oysters (the best in the country), geoduck, razor clams,
Manila clams, mussels, squid, Dungeness crab, and the list goes on. Although we have great fish and shellfish,
I wish we could take a page from the East Coast in one respect. We tend to either fry our seafood or gussy it up,
with very little in between. Would that there were more places that steamed or boiled the beasties of the sea and
then dumped them out on newspaper with some crackers on the side. Eating with your hands and really tasting
what you're eating—that's a good model to emulate.

That said, the Italians know a thing or two about fish themselves. Roasting a fish whole on the bone, scent-
ing it with lemon and thyme, and filleting it at the table is a fabulous way to eat as well. So is wrapping soft-shell
crab in prosciutto and giving it a quick sear. The recipes that follow range from steamed clams accented with
cured pork cheek to more complicated preparations such as Seared Scallops with Chanterelles and Parsnip and
Pear Purée (page 177). As with the crudos in "Nibbles and Bits," what they all have in common is a commitment
to allowing the flavor and texture of the fish or seafood to truly shine.

Grilled Sardines with Baby Fennel, Capers, and Taggiasca Olives

This is a dish to transport you to the Italian Riviera—the freshest sardines, simply grilled, splashed with lemon, briny olives, and the sweet anise flavor of the season's first fennel. This is also finger food, so get out a big stack of napkins and don't eat them with those who are excessively dainty. They don't deserve them anyway. It would play into the whole relaxed-by-the-sea thing if you have your fishmonger scale and clean the sardines.

2 heads baby fennel

$1/2$ cup pitted Taggiasca olives, halved

$1/4$ cup salt-packed capers, soaked in water for 30 minutes and drained

Juice of 2 lemons (about $1/4$ cup)

$1/4$ cup lightly packed fresh parsley leaves

12 fresh sardines, scaled and gutted

$1/4$ cup extra-virgin olive oil

Kosher salt and freshly ground pepper

Trim the root ends of the fennel and peel them with a vegetable peeler. Slice crosswise as thinly as possible. Combine the fennel with the olives, capers, lemon juice, and parsley and allow to marinate while you prepare the sardines.

Preheat the grill on high. Brush the sardines with the olive oil and season generously with salt and pepper. Place on a hot grill and cook for 2 to 3 minutes per side, or until the flesh easily pulls away from the bones. Divide the sardines among 4 plates and spoon the relish over the top, along with any accumulated juices.

Mob-Hit Squid

Though this recipe sounds straight out of a Coen brothers' movie, the name refers to the fact that you chop off the squids' arms and stuff them inside their own bodies. Trust me—this is my kind of punishment. I use cooked Controne beans as a binder instead of bread-crumbs, ensuring the filling is creamy and light, and I add slab bacon for a hit of smoke and texture. When you grill the tentacles, remember that you're just precooking them and don't leave them on the heat too long. Another key to this dish is ensuring that your filling is at room temperature before you stuff the squid. If it's too cold, you'll overcook the bodies while you heat the stuffing through. If you want to stuff the squid earlier in the day, just take them out of the fridge about a half hour before grilling.

1 cup Controne Beans (page 162)

2 tablespoons chopped fresh parsley

2 tablespoons extra-virgin olive oil, plus more for rubbing

8 large squid, cleaned

1/2 pound Home-Cured Bacon (page 146), diced

Kosher salt and freshly ground pepper

Preheat the grill on high.

Pulse the beans in a food processor into a rough purée, then place in a bowl with the parsley and the olive oil.

Cut the tentacles off the squid bodies in one piece, keeping the legs intact and creating a large opening at the bottom of each squid body. Grill, turning once, until the tentacles are just cooked through, about 2 minutes per side. Transfer to a cutting board and give the tentacles a rough chop. Add the grilled tentacles to the bowl with the bean purée.

Place the bacon in a sauté pan over medium to medium-low heat and cook for 4 to 6 minutes, or until the bacon slightly crisps and renders some of its fat. Drain the bacon and add to the rest of the ingredients. Mix gently but thoroughly with a rubber spatula. Season with salt and pepper.

To stuff the squid, you can use a pastry bag fitted with a large tip, a resealable bag with a corner cut off, or a small spoon. Fill the bodies loosely because the stuffing will expand during cooking. After filling, close the top of each squid by threading a toothpick through twice.

Rub each body with olive oil and season with salt and pepper. Grill the squid until the bodies are opaque and the filling is heated through, 6 to 8 minutes.

Fluke with Radish and Citrus Relish

Fluke—often called "summer flounder" on the East Coast or hirame in Japan—is an extremely light and delicate fish. Because of its mild flavor, I like to pair it with this citrus relish, complementing, but not overpowering, the fish's characteristics. For the baby leaves, you can use arugula, Italian parsley, microgreens, or whatever you can find and like. Feel free to vary the citrus in the relish as well, experimenting with grapefruit, blood oranges, or sweet Cara Cara oranges in the winter. Because fluke cooks so quickly, have your relish ready before you begin the fish. To make sure you get a nice crispy exterior on the fillets, use two sauté pans if necessary. Crowding the pan will cause the fish to steam instead of sear.

RELISH

1 Meyer lemon

8 radishes, trimmed and cut into eighths

1 orange

2 tablespoons extra-virgin olive oil

Kosher salt and freshly ground pepper

2 tablespoons extra-virgin olive oil

4 (4-ounce) fluke fillets

Kosher salt

1 cup baby leaves (see headnote)

To make the relish, lay the lemon on its side and cut off a thin slice from the top and bottom of the fruit, then stand it on a flat end. Using a sharp knife and following the curve of the fruit, slice down the sides of the lemon, removing all the peel and pith as you go. Once the peel and pith are removed, hold the lemon in your palm. Cut along the membrane on each side of the individual sections and allow the flesh to fall free onto a cutting board. When the lemon is sectioned, chop coarsely and place in a bowl with the radishes. Squeeze the sectioned lemon in the bowl to catch all the juice. Repeat with the orange. Add the olive oil to the bowl and toss to combine. Season with salt and pepper and set aside.

Using 1 large sauté pan or 2 smaller pans, heat the olive oil over high heat until almost smoking. Season the fluke fillets with salt and add to the hot pan or pans. Sear for 2 to 3 minutes on the first side or until golden brown, then flip and cook for about 1 minute on the second side, until just brown.

Divide the radish and citrus relish, along with a spoonful of liquid, among 4 deep, wide bowls. Sprinkle one-quarter of the baby greens into each bowl and place a fillet of on top of each. Drizzle a little more of the vinaigrette from the relish on top and serve.

Ode to the Northwest (with a Nod to Cincinnati)

It's spring in Seattle—that means fresh, tender peas, the first succulent morels, and firm, snowy halibut begging to swim around in a bowl with all that other goodness. For a little bite, I add some shaved Cincinnati radish—a long, mild radish that looks like a baby carrot. This is a lovely dish that puts me in mind of longer, warmer days.

2 tablespoons unsalted butter

4 ounces morels, cleaned and halved lengthwise (see page 64)

1 cup shucked, blanched English peas

Kosher salt and freshly ground pepper

2 tablespoons minced chives

4 (4-ounce) halibut fillets

2 tablespoons extra-virgin olive oil, plus more for drizzling

4 Cincinnati radishes, shaved with a mandoline

Preheat the oven to 400°F.

Heat the butter in a sauté pan over medium heat and add the mushrooms. Sauté the mushrooms until soft, 2 to 3 minutes, then add the peas. Toss to warm through. Season with salt and pepper and add the chives. Keep warm.

Pat the fish fillets dry and season both sides with salt and pepper. In a large ovenproof sauté pan over high heat, heat the olive oil until it just starts to smoke. Add the fillets and turn off the heat. Give the pan a wiggle to make sure there is oil under all of the fillets. Turn the heat back on to high. Sear until golden brown on one side, 3 to 4 minutes, turn the fish, and then transfer the pan to the oven. Roast for 3 to 4 minutes, or until barely cooked through.

Put a mound of mushroom mixture in each of 4 warmed bowls. Top each with a halibut fillet and sprinkle the radishes over the top. Drizzle with olive oil and serve.

Roasted Skate Wing with Brown Butter and Potatoes

Although skate "wing" might sound exotic, skate is nothing more than a kissing cousin to sharks, as well as a delicious fish with delicately flavored, sweet white meat. It's more prevalent on the East Coast; out West, you will probably need to ask your fishmonger to order it for you. Weighting the skate while it cooks keeps it from curling, making for even cooking and a nicer presentation. Be careful when you add the wine to the brown butter, because the mixture will bubble up and spit a little.

1 pound Piccolo potatoes

4 (6-ounce) fillets peeled skate wing, bone in

Kosher salt and freshly ground pepper

2 tablespoons extra-virgin olive oil

6 tablespoons unsalted butter

1/4 cup white wine

2 tablespoons chopped fresh parsley

Preheat the oven to 400°F.

Place the potatoes in a large pot and cover with cool water by 1 inch. Bring to a boil and cook for about 15 minutes, or until just tender when pierced with a knife.

When the potatoes have cooked for about 10 minutes, season the skate wing fillets with salt and pepper. Place a large, ovenproof sauté pan over high heat and add the olive oil. When the oil is just smoking, add the skate wings and place a small weight, such as a heavy pot lid, on top. Cook for 3 minutes on the first side, or until golden brown. Remove the weight, flip the fillets, and place the pan in the oven. Roast for 4 to 5 minutes, or until the flesh easily flakes off the bone.

Drain the potatoes and reserve. Melt the butter in a sauté pan over medium heat and continue cooking until the butter turns nut brown and becomes quite fragrant. Be careful that it doesn't burn; the line between nutty and black is a fine one. Immediately pour in the wine and swirl to combine. Decrease the heat to low and add the potatoes to the pan, cooking gently until warmed through. Season to taste with salt and pepper. Add the parsley, toss, and spoon the mixture over the skate. Serve.

Black Bass with Thyme, Lemon, and Garlic

There's nothing fancy about a whole, roasted fish—it's just good. While the fish cooks, the herbs and lemon perfume the flesh, and the fish turns out moist and succulent with crisp skin. It doesn't get much better. If you can't find black bass, branzino, snapper, or rockfish would also work.

This recipe is for one whole fish, but it's just as easy to double the recipe if you're having friends to dinner. Roast off a couple of fish, add a couple of other dishes, and let everyone share.

1 lemon, thinly sliced

1 whole black bass (about 1 pound),
gutted and scaled

3 large cloves garlic, smashed

3 sprigs parsley

1 bunch thyme

Kosher salt and freshly ground pepper

2 tablespoons extra-virgin olive oil, plus more
for drizzling

Preheat the oven to 450°F.

Place 3 or 4 lemon slices in the cavity of the fish. Add 1 garlic clove, the parsley, and a few sprigs of thyme. Cut 3 equal pieces of kitchen twine and tie the fish shut. Use scissors or your knife to remove any excess string. Season the fish liberally with salt and pepper.

Heat the olive oil in your largest ovenproof skillet until almost smoking. (If you're cooking 2 fish at once, your pan must be at least 12 inches in diameter.) Put the fish in the pan on its belly, as though it's swimming again. Brown for 3 minutes. Flip onto one side and brown, then flip the fish over and cook until golden, 3 to 4 minutes. Put the remaining 2 garlic cloves and a few sprigs of thyme in the pan and slip into the oven.

Roast for 8 to 10 minutes, flipping the fish halfway through the cooking time. When done the flesh should pull easily off of the bone. Remove the fish from the pan, discarding the herbs and garlic.

Run a sharp knife along the spine on one side. Insert a small spatula or table knife into the incision and pry the fillet up and off the bones. Turn the fish over and repeat. Drizzle the flesh with olive oil, sprinkle with salt, and serve

Poached Black Bass with Spring Garlic and Mint

At once light and intensely flavorful, poaching with aromatics is a wonderful treatment for black bass. Here, I use spring garlic and onions, but the recipe is easily adaptable to other times of the year. Make sure you use some member of the onion family for flavor; in winter, add shaved radish, fennel . . . use your imagination. This dish goes quickly if you have your fishmonger do the work for you; just ask for the trimmings to take home for making the fumet.

2 tablespoons extra-virgin olive oil

2 baby leeks, sliced and rinsed well

2 spring onions, thinly sliced

1 stalk spring garlic, thinly sliced

2 cups Fish Fumet (recipe follows)

2 whole black bass (1 to 1¼ pounds), gutted, scaled, and filleted

Kosher salt and freshly ground pepper

8 fresh mint leaves, chopped

2 tablespoons minced chives

½ lemon

2 tablespoons best-quality olive oil

Pour the olive oil into a wide, high-sided sauté pan and add the leeks, onions, and garlic. Sauté over medium heat until soft but not colored. Add the Fish Fumet and bring to a boil, then decrease the heat to keep at a bare simmer.

Season the fillets with salt and pepper and place in the poaching liquid, skin-side up. The liquid should come about halfway up the fish fillets. Using a spoon, baste the tops of the fillets with the Fumet as they cook. The fillets will begin to curl, but continue basting, keeping the broth evenly coating the skin of the fish. Cook in this manner, basting continuously, for 4 to 5 minutes, or until the skin pulls away from the fillets easily. You can remove the skin if you like, though it looks pretty and tastes good.

Remove the fillets from the liquid and divide among 4 warmed bowls. Keep the Fumet and the aromatics simmering on the stove. Add the mint leaves and chives to the Fumet. Squeeze in the lemon juice, and add the best-quality olive oil, and swirl to blend. Check the seasonings. Spoon the Fish Fumet over the fillets, making sure each bowl has vegetables and herbs.

FISH FUMET

Bones from 1 whole black bass

1 cup water

1 cup wine

3 stalks celery

1 clove garlic

1 small onion, halved horizontally

1 leek

Place all of the ingredients in a stockpot over high heat. Bring to a boil, reduce the heat, and simmer for 45 minutes. Strain.

Seared Scallops with Chanterelles and Parsnip and Pear Purée

This beautiful fall dish is a study in silken textures, from the velvety purée to the creamy interior of the ivory scallops. Quick searing gives the scallops a crispy, caramelized exterior that is well matched to the sweetness of the pear in the purée, while the chanterelles add texture, depth, and a luscious, buttery flavor. Although there are three separate parts to this recipe, it's still relatively straightforward to prepare. Make the purée first, then hold it at room temperature; the searing and sautéing take no more than five minutes.

PURÉE

1 pound parsnips

1/2 pound pears (about 1 large Bosc pear)

2 cups milk

1/4 pound fresh chanterelle mushrooms

2 tablespoons unsalted butter

1 tablespoon chopped fresh parsley

Kosher salt and freshly ground pepper

2 tablespoons extra-virgin olive oil, plus more for drizzling

12 sea scallops

Aged balsamic vinegar, for drizzling

To make the purée, peel the parsnips and quarter them lengthwise, removing as much core as you can. Discard the cores and roughly chop the remainder. Peel the pears, core, and roughly chop.

Place the parsnips in a saucepan and cover with milk. Bring to a boil over high heat, then decrease the heat and simmer until very tender, about 8 minutes. Add the pear and cook for 2 minutes longer, or until the pear is soft.

Drain off the milk and purée the mixture in a blender until smooth. Place in a bowl, cover, and set aside.

Wipe the mushrooms clean with a damp cloth and quarter them if large. Heat the butter in a sauté pan over medium-high heat and add the mushrooms. Cook until the mushrooms are tender and have rendered their juices. Add the parsley to the pan and toss. Season to taste with salt and pepper.

Heat the olive oil in a sauté pan over high heat. Pat the scallops dry and season on both sides with salt and pepper. Sear on both sides until crispy, browned, and heated through, 2 to 3 minutes per side.

Spoon about 2 tablespoons of the purée onto each of 4 plates, spreading it out into a thin puddle. Top each with one-quarter of the mushrooms and any accumulated juices. Place 3 scallops on each plate on top of the mushrooms. Drizzle with the olive oil and a few drops aged balsamic vinegar. Serve.

Steamed Clams with Guanciale and Sorrel

I love it when the first bunches of springtime sorrel appear in the market. It has a fantastic sour, lemony-mint thing going on that does something great for clams. The only drawback is that when you cook sorrel, it turns the worst color of brown. Sprinkle it on the dish at the last minute for the best flavor and look. Please try to find *guanciale* for this dish—it has a delightful fattiness to it that can't really be replicated. If you can't find *guanciale,* use bacon or pancetta instead. Everyone thinks clams have to be cooked over high heat. It's not necessary in order for the clams to open, and it can render them tough if not done carefully.

8 ounces *guanciale*

2 tablespoons extra-virgin olive oil

4 cloves garlic, sliced paper-thin

1 teaspoon chile flakes

2 pounds Manila clams

1/2 cup white wine

Juice of 1 lemon

5 sorrel leaves, cut into a chiffonade

In a large saucepan over medium heat, brown the *guanciale* to render some of the fat. Pour off the fat and add the olive oil. Add the garlic and chile flakes and cook until the garlic is soft and the chile flakes are toasted, 2 minutes. Add the clams and increase the heat to medium-high. Add the wine and cover.

After 5 or 6 minutes, check to see whether the clams have opened. Discard any that have failed to open. Add the lemon juice and toss. Pile into a serving bowl and top with the sorrel. Serve immediately.

Prosciutto-Wrapped Soft-Shell Crab Cigars with Shaved Radish and Arugula Salad

SERVES 4

Although these savory, salty little bundles are a little too fat to truly resemble cigars, rolling the crabs in the prosciutto does employ a technique used by skilled workers in Cuba. It might also seem familiar to you if you've ever hand-rolled anything in papers. For directions on cleaning the soft-shell crabs, see page 32. Make sure you go easy on the salt in this dish because the prosciutto already contains plenty.

4 (3- to 4-ounce) soft-shell crabs, cleaned

Kosher salt and freshly cracked pepper

4 long slices prosciutto

3 tablespoons extra-virgin olive oil, plus more for drizzling

12 French breakfast radishes, trimmed and shaved with a mandoline

2 cups loosely packed baby arugula leaves

1 teaspoon fresh lemon juice

Season the crabs lightly with salt and pepper on both sides. Lay out the slices of prosciutto with the short end facing you. Place a crab on each of the short ends and roll up, tucking in the claws as you go.

In a large sauté pan over high heat, heat 2 tablespoons of the olive oil. Add the wrapped crabs and sear for about 2 minutes per side, until the prosciutto is crispy and the crabs are cooked through.

Dress the radishes and arugula leaves with the remaining 1 tablespoon olive oil and the lemon juice, seasoning to taste with salt and pepper.

Divide the salad among 4 plates, mounding it slightly. Place a cooked, wrapped crab on top of each. Drizzle with olive oil and serve.

ETHAN STOWELL'S NEW ITALIAN KITCHEN

Grilled Mackerel with Crispy Potatoes and Caper and Preserved Lemon Sauce

Mackerel is a rich fish with fabulous texture and depth of flavor. Though it's not traditional, preserved lemon adds a piquant, salty touch to a rustic pounded sauce. To make sure the potatoes are crispy when you serve the dish, grill the fish first and fry the potatoes right before serving. Parboiling the potatoes makes it easy to get them crispy, while ensuring they're cooked through.

4 tablespoons salt-packed capers, soaked in water for 30 minutes and drained

4 anchovy fillets

$1/2$ Preserved Lemon, rind only (page 218)

1 small clove garlic

$3/4$ cup extra-virgin olive oil, plus more for brushing and drizzling

4 (3-ounce) mackerel fillets, skin on

Kosher salt and freshly ground pepper

$3/4$ pound small Yukon Gold potatoes, parboiled and thickly sliced

Using a mortar and pestle or a food processor, mix together the capers, anchovies, Preserved Lemon, garlic, and $1/2$ cup of the olive oil until a chunky but emulsified sauce is formed. Set aside.

Heat a grill or grill pan over high heat. Season the fish fillets on both sides with salt and pepper and brush with olive oil. Place the fish in the pan, skin-side down, and cook until the skin is crispy, about 3 minutes. Carefully flip the fish and cook on the second side for about 2 minutes, or until the fish is cooked through. Transfer to a plate while you fry the potatoes.

In a large sauté pan, or 2 smaller pans, heat the remaining $1/4$ cup olive oil over high heat until the oil is nearly smoking. Add the potatoes and fry until crispy and golden brown, 1 to 2 minutes per side. Drain briefly on paper towels to absorb the excess oil.

Spread 1 tablespoon of the lemon sauce on each of 4 plates. Fan out the potatoes in an overlapping line on top of the sauce, making sure some of the sauce peeks out around the edges. Place the fish on top, drizzle with olive oil, and serve.

Cheese for the Civilized and Desserts for the Rest of You

It is true that I rarely have dessert when I eat out. For me, it's just a little over the top. Philosophically, I part ways with these places that conclude your dinner with a plate filled with fanciful concoctions topped with sprinkles and crunchies and wafers and genoise and ganache and foam and . . . you get my point. That said, a beautifully made, straightforward dessert can be a lovely ending to a meal, and there are a number of great recipes in this chapter for those of you who crave a little something sweet. I'm not anti-dessert; I just like what I like. And at the end of a meal, generally speaking, I like cheese.

Some people are purists and won't serve bread with their cheese. I do. Peasant bread, artisanal bread. I don't want crackers or sourdough—that's just not okay. A nice baguette, though, that's a good starting place. A good raisin-pecan or walnut could work its way in there, depending on what you're serving. And my personal favorite way to have a cheese course is with a nice little salad. Cheese courses should be easy to prepare and relatively simple, but the accompaniment should add another dimension to the cheese, revealing its very best characteristics.

The cheeses I feature in this chapter are all Italian and are some of my favorites. But cheese is a very personal issue, I find, so do your research. I don't mean the kind that involves a library; I promise, this will be fun. Find a local cheese shop or even a gourmet market with a large selection and knowledgeable staff. Ask for tastes and buy what you like, and please, please don't serve your cheese cold. Refrigeration is a wonderful advent in food preservation, but it blunts the flavor and affects the texture of every cheese you buy. Simply leave it on the counter during your meal and it should come to temperature by the time you're ready to eat it.

For those of you who choose the sweeter path, there are some treasures here. In the restaurants, we usually have one or two offerings—maybe a cherry-grappa ice cream or a peach sorbet. They aren't overly complicated, but they are perfectly what they are. That philosophy, an Italian way of eating that I admire, is reflected here. From twists on beloved favorites—such as Chocolate Ice Cream (page 195), Zabaglione with Mixed Berries (page 203), or cookies that taste like nonna's scraps of sugared pie dough—to elegant Rhubarb Soup with Prosecco (page 192) or Espresso Granita with Grappa Cream (page 204), these are focused, concentrated desserts. The Blueberry-Basil Sorbet (page 202) is at once savory and intense, but the flavors are pure; the Toasted Walnut Ice Cream (page 196) captures the essence of roasting nuts. Yes, the title of the chapter pokes a little fun, but I promise I will not judge you if you make one or all of the dessert recipes that follow; in fact, I'd probably join you in a nibble, or a spoonful, or a bowl.

My profound thanks to Eli Dahlin, a talented and underutilized pastry chef at How to Cook a Wolf, who helped to develop and test the desserts.

Goat Cheese with Chestnut Honey and Hazelnut Dust

Go to your farmers' market and get the freshest and best goat cheese you can find—the tang and texture are critical with a dish this straightforward. Chestnut honey has an earthiness, almost a gaminess, really, that adds depth and structure to the dish.

4 ounces fresh goat cheese

Chestnut honey, for drizzling

2 tablespoons ground or finely chopped hazelnuts

Form the goat cheese into 4 quenelles using 2 soup spoons, scooping the cheese out of one and rounding it as you pass the cheese back and forth to form a smooth football shape. Arrange on a plate and drizzle with the honey. Put the nuts in a sieve and dust the plate.

Ginepro with Gin-Soaked Pear

A cheese course for gin lovers, Ginepro is a sheep's milk pecorino from Emilia-Romagna that is first rubbed with balsamic vinegar and olive oil and then buried in juniper berries. It's a salty, herbal cheese with an awesome tang. To complement the flavor and amp up the juniper, caramelize some pears and flame them with gin, then allow them to macerate to develop the flavor. With that much gin going on, pour a dry prosecco to drink with it.

$^1/_4$ cup water

$^1/_4$ cup sugar

$^1/_2$ cup plus 1 teaspoon high-quality gin

2 Bosc pears, peeled, cored, and diced

$^1/_2$ teaspoon peppercorns

8 ounces Ginepro

Combine the water and sugar in a saucepan over medium-high heat and cook, stirring occasionally, until the sugar dissolves and the mixture turns into a light caramel. Remove the pan from the heat and add $^1/_2$ cup of the gin. Light the gin and allow it to flame for a minute or two. Put the saucepan over low heat, add the pears, and toss to coat. Turn the pears out into a bowl and stir in the peppercorns. Sprinkle the mixture with the remaining 1 teaspoon gin. Let macerate for at least 24 hours, covered, at room temperature before serving with the Ginepro.

La Tur with Oven-Roasted Tomato Petals

One of my favorite cheeses from Piedmont, you can tell La Tur is special from the moment you see the little round presented in its ruffled paper wrapper. This is a very well-balanced cheese, young, made from goat, sheep, and cow's milk. Cutting through the soft rind you find a slightly tangy, nearly mousselike interior, and each round feeds four perfectly. Roasted tomato "petals" make a colorful and velvety pairing, richly drizzled with the best balsamic you can afford. If you can buy 100-year-old balsamic, do it—celebrate your good fortune. If, like me, you can only afford something a bit younger, don't let it hold you back from ending an evening with this dish. Serve with a plain baguette or slices of peasant bread; nut- or herb-flavored breads will compete with the flavors.

4 large, ripe beefsteak tomatoes (about 2 pounds)

2 sprigs thyme

2 cloves garlic, thinly sliced

2 tablespoons extra-virgin olive oil

Kosher salt and freshly ground pepper

1 (8-ounce) round La Tur

Best-quality aged balsamic vinegar, for drizzling

Preheat the oven to 300°F.

Bring a large pot of water to a rapid boil and prepare an ice-water bath in a large bowl. Core the tomatoes and cut an X in the skin at the bottom of each one. Blanch the tomatoes in the boiling water for 30 to 60 seconds. The skin should easily pull back from the X. Immediately plunge into the ice bath. Once the skin cools it should easily pull away from the fruit. Using your fingers or a paring knife, skin the tomatoes and cut into eighths. Remove the seeds and inner flesh. You should be left with soft, peeled "petals." Place the petals in a bowl.

Remove the leaves from the thyme sprigs and add to the tomatoes. Add the garlic to the bowl along with the olive oil, a pinch of salt, and a grinding of pepper. Toss to coat, then place the petals on a wire rack set over a foil-lined baking sheet. Roast for 2 hours, or until the tomatoes are slightly shriveled and the juices have concentrated. Allow to cool to room temperature.

Cut the cheese into quarters and place on individual plates. Scatter a few petals across the plate and drizzle with a tiny bit of aged balsamic.

Lemon Verbena Panna Cotta with Poached Peaches

There are fruit people, and there are chocolate people. Even chocolate people will lick their plates clean when presented with a refreshing, lemony panna cotta strewn with wine-steeped peaches. Panna cotta makes a nice spring and summertime dessert because it's not so rich that you leave the table feeling stuffed, and the lemon verbena adds a welcome, herbaceous tang. This dish is perfect for company because the panna cotta must be made ahead, and the peaches "cook" while coming to room temperature.

2$^1/_2$ cups whipping cream

$^1/_2$ cup sugar

$^1/_2$ cup crème fraîche or Greek-style yogurt

$^1/_4$ teaspoon Kosher salt

10 fresh lemon verbena leaves

1$^3/_4$ cups whole milk

1 ($^1/_4$-ounce) packet powdered, unflavored gelatin

1 fresh egg

Poached Peaches, for accompaniment (recipe follows)

Combine the cream, sugar, crème fraîche, and salt in a saucepan and bring to a boil over medium heat. Remove from the heat and add the lemon verbena, lightly crushing the leaves before adding them to the pot. Allow the mixture to steep for about 1 hour. Keep tasting as it steeps until it has the flavor you want.

Meanwhile, pour the milk into a bowl. Add the gelatin and whisk until it dissolves. Add the egg and beat well.

Once the cream mixture has steeped, rewarm it over low heat until it reaches a low simmer, then pour over the milk-gelatin mixture and whisk until completely combined. Let the mixture sit for 5 minutes, then pour through a fine-mesh sieve into a heatproof container with a pouring spout.

Lightly grease 10 ramekins, plastic cups, or coffee cups and line them up on a baking sheet. Divide the mixture among the ramekins and put in the fridge. Chill until set, about 4 hours. Serve with Poached Peaches.

POACHED PEACHES

2 large peaches

$^1/_2$ cup sugar

2 cups rosé wine

1 vanilla bean, scraped

$^1/_2$ whole nutmeg

Set a large pot of water on the stove to boil and prepare an ice-water bath in a bowl large enough to hold the peaches. When the water comes to a boil, scald the peaches for 30 seconds. Using a mesh sieve or slotted spoon, transfer the fruit immediately to the ice-water bath to stop the cooking. Using a paring knife, peel the peaches (the skins should now slip off easily) and put the peels in a saucepan. Slice the peaches into eighths and place in a heatproof bowl.

Add the sugar, wine, vanilla, and nutmeg to the saucepan and set over high heat. Bring the mixture to a boil and continue cooking for 5 minutes longer. Pour the boiling mixture over the peaches and set the fruit aside to cool and macerate in the spiced wine. Serve with the panna cotta.

Robiola with Gooseberry Compote

I think of Robiola as what I always want Brie to be. It's even more lush than that French imposter, with a smooth, flowing core that's like pure silk. The very best specimens must be tasted in Italy, where they don't let unpasteurized milk stand between any man and his cheese. We get very fine imports here, however, and depending on the producer, your Robiola may be fashioned from either goat, sheep, or cow's milk, or a combination. Because Robiola is so rich, I like to pair it with something tart and jammy, like this easy gooseberry compote. To serve, make sure the compote has cooled completely and the Robiola is at room temperature to allow it to be its runny, best self.

1/4 cup water

1/4 cup sugar

1 pint gooseberries

Squeeze of lemon

Pinch of Kosher salt

4 ounces Robiola

Combine the water and sugar in a saucepan, place over medium-high heat, and cook, stirring occasionally, until the sugar dissolves and the mixture turns into a light caramel. Add the gooseberries, lemon juice, and salt. Continue to cook over medium heat until you have a nice, thick syrup and the berries begin to burst, 3 to 4 minutes. Scrape into a bowl and allow to cool to room temperature.

Scoop 2 tablespoons of the gooseberry compote onto each of 4 plates and serve with the Robiola.

Cacio Faenum with Baked Apricot and Almond Purée

Cacio Faenum is a fragrant sheep's milk cheese that, like little baby Jesus, is lovingly laid on a bed of hay to rest. Unlike the newborn king, however, the cheese is actually wrapped in dried grass and buried in a hay-filled barrel for a little more than a month. You'll recognize this incredible cheese by its charming hay wrapper and a grassy, barn-y fragrance that marries nicely with the earthiness of apricots and almonds.

Extra-virgin olive oil, for coating and drizzling

4 ripe apricots, halved and pitted

1 teaspoon sugar

1/2 cup Marcona almonds, toasted

8 ounces Cacio Faenum

Preheat the oven to 400°F.

Place a silicone liner on a baking sheet and coat with a little olive oil. Roll the apricots around in the oil, then place them, cut-sides down, on the liner. Sprinkle the tops with sugar.

Bake for about 15 minutes, or until the tops are brown and the halves collapse. Transfer to a plate and allow to cool to room temperature. Place in the bowl of a food processor along with the almonds, and purée until very smooth. Push the purée through a fine-mesh sieve to ensure it is perfectly silky and smooth.

Smear about 2 tablespoons purée on each plate and serve alongside a wedge of Cacio Faenum. Drizzle both with olive oil and serve.

Rhubarb Soup with Prosecco

Rhubarb is one of those love-hate foods. For me, it's all about the love. Not only do I like the tartness, a zinging alternative to too-cloying desserts, but it's pretty, too. Yes, it's pink and it's pretty and I'm secure enough to admit it. With the gentle bubbles emanating from the prosecco, this soup is impressive enough to end a fancy spring meal, and it's easy, to boot.

2 pounds rhubarb (about 6 large stalks)

1 cup sugar

$1/2$ cup dry prosecco

4 teaspoons plain, Greek-style yogurt

2 tablespoons crushed toasted pistachios

4 sprigs mint, for garnish (optional)

Cut the rhubarb crosswise into $1/2$-inch slices and toss with the sugar. Macerate for at least 1 hour, preferably overnight. Place in a heatproof bowl or double boiler and heat slowly over simmering water. Cook, stirring occasionally, for about 20 minutes, or until the rhubarb is soft and has given up its juices. You want the rhubarb to be tender but still maintain its shape.

Pour the mixture into a fine-mesh sieve set over a bowl and strain out all the liquid. Reserve about 3 nicely shaped slices of rhubarb for each serving, then put the remaining fruit through a food mill.

In the end, you should end up with about 1 cup each of juice and purée. Combine the two and set in the fridge to chill thoroughly.

Right before serving, add the prosecco.

For each serving, measure out $1/2$ cup soup and place in a bowl. Decorate the top with reserved slices of rhubarb. Dollop 1 teaspoon of yogurt into each bowl, and sprinkle with $1/2$ tablespoon of the pistachios. Garnish with mint if you like.

Roasted Figs with Chocolate-Espresso Ganache

This dessert is layered with toasty, earthy flavors, from the concentrated sweetness of the roasted figs to the nutty brown butter to the chocolate ganache deepened with a touch of coffee. You can ride the sweet-salty wave by sprinkling with a finishing salt at the end, or simply dust with powdered sugar. You can't go wrong.

GANACHE

8 ounces semisweet chocolate, chopped

4 shots espresso, or $1/2$ cup extra-strong coffee

$1/4$ cup sugar

Pinch of Kosher salt

2 tablespoons heavy cream

FIGS

2 tablespoons Brown Butter (recipe follows)

$1/4$ cup honey

Pinch of Kosher salt

2 pints figs, halved lengthwise

Confectioners' sugar, for dusting

Fleur de sel (optional)

6 to 12 fresh mint leaves, for garnish

Preheat the oven to 300°F.

To make the ganache, combine the chocolate, espresso, sugar and salt in a double boiler and heat over barely simmering water. Whisk until smooth. Add the heavy cream and transfer to the refrigerator to cool.

To make the figs, combine the Brown Butter, honey, and Kosher salt in a bowl and toss with the figs to coat. Place the figs on a parchment-lined baking sheet and drizzle with any remaining syrup. Bake for about $1^1/2$ hours, or until completely soft and slightly dry. Baste with any remaining juices.

To serve, puddle about 2 tablespoons ganache on each of 6 plates and smear lightly across the dish. Top with the figs, about 3 per person. Dust with confectioners' sugar. Add a generous sprinkle of fleur de sel, if you like, and garnish with a mint leaf or two.

BROWN BUTTER

1 stick unsalted butter

Place the butter in a cold saucepan and set on the stove over medium heat. It will soon begin to melt and sizzle. After the butter melts completely, 2 to 3 minutes, it will begin to foam as the milk solids separate out. As these solids drop to the bottom of the pan, they will toast and the butter will take on a brownish color and a toasty aroma. Watch the heat carefully during this time to make sure the solids do not burn, lowering the heat if needed. When the butter stops foaming and is a light brown color, remove immediately from the heat and pour through a sieve or a coffee filter to separate out the solids, which you can discard.

This will make more brown butter than you need for the figs. Try tossing it with vegetables or drizzling over fish. It will keep, covered, in the refrigerator for up to 2 weeks.

Chocolate Ice Cream

This is not the chocolate ice cream you used to eat as a kid, though no kid would say no to a big, fat dish of it. This has more depth thanks to brown sugar, and the tang of crème fraîche takes the edge off the sweetness. For an elegant richness, use the very best semisweet chocolate you can find. Please, no chocolate chips. Not only would the flavor suffer, but the emulsifiers added to chocolate chips would ruin the texture of the dessert.

2 cups heavy cream

2 cups milk

1¹/₄ cups packed brown sugar

1 teaspoon Kosher salt

¹/₈ teaspoon ground cinnamon

8 large fresh egg yolks, at room temperature

¹/₃ cup cocoa powder (not Dutch process)

8 ounces semisweet chocolate, chopped

¹/₂ cup crème fraîche or sour cream

¹/₄ teaspoon pure vanilla extract

Combine the cream, milk, brown sugar, salt, and cinnamon in a large saucepan and bring to a boil. Place the egg yolks in a large heatproof bowl. Add about ¹/₂ cup of the boiling mixture to the egg yolks and whisk furiously. Add another ¹/₂ cup, whisk, then add all of the cream mixture to the yolks and whisk until completely combined and smooth.

Place the cocoa powder and chocolate pieces in another large bowl, then add the cream mixture in three batches, whisking until smooth after each addition. Once the chocolate is completely incorporated, whisk in the crème fraîche and vanilla.

Cool the mixture in an ice-water bath, then pour into an ice cream maker and freeze according to the manufacturer's directions.

Toasted Walnut Ice Cream

Rich and earthy, with a haunting flavor that comes from steeping toasted walnuts in cream before making your custard, this makes a very elegant finish to a meal (and it's good straight from the freezer at midnight, too).

3 cups heavy cream

2 cups milk

1 teaspoon Kosher salt

1 pound shelled walnuts

8 large fresh egg yolks, at room temperature

1 cup sugar

Preheat the oven to 325°F.

Heat the cream, milk, and salt in a large saucepan over low heat.

Spread the walnuts on a baking sheet and toast until fragrant, about 10 minutes. As you pull the nuts out of the oven, turn the heat under the cream-milk mixture to high and bring to a boil. Turn off the heat and add the nuts while they are still warm. Allow the walnuts to steep in the cream and milk for at least 1 hour, or overnight for best flavor. Strain the mixture through a fine-mesh sieve into a clean saucepan and discard the nuts. Place the egg yolks in a large heatproof bowl.

Add the sugar to the cream mixture and bring to a boil. Add about $1/2$ cup of the boiling mixture to the egg yolks and whisk furiously. Add another $1/2$ cup, whisk, then add all of the cream mixture to the yolks and whisk until completely combined and smooth.

Pour the mixture through a fine-mesh sieve into a bowl, cover, and refrigerate until cold. Pour into an ice cream maker and freeze according to the manufacturer's directions.

Pear–Star Anise Ice Cream

I can't decide whether I love the color—a pale celadon—or the exotic flavor of this ice cream more. The pear causes the base to have a thinner consistency than some other ice creams have before freezing, but the final texture is lovely. It's hard to peg the flavor as star anise in the ice cream, because the spice mellows with the cold and the cream, but it's addictive. This isn't a scoop-in-a-cone kind of dessert, but an elegant cookie on the side would be nice.

2 cups heavy cream

2 cups milk

1 teaspoon Kosher salt

1 cup sugar

6 pods star anise, crushed

8 ripe pears, such as Bartlett

8 large fresh egg yolks, at room temperature

1/4 teaspoon pure vanilla extract

Combine the cream, milk, salt, and sugar in a large saucepan and bring to a boil. Add the star anise and immediately remove from the heat. Allow the cream mixture to steep for about 30 minutes.

Stem and core the pears, then pulse in the food processor until you get a chunky purée. Strain the purée by pushing through a fine-mesh sieve, pressing on the solids with a spatula or the bottom of a ladle. You should end up with about 2 cups of liquid. Discard the solids. Put the pear liquid in a saucepan and cook over high heat, stirring frequently, until reduced by half, about 10 minutes.

Add the pear syrup to the cream mixture and bring to a boil over high heat.

While that mixture heats, place the egg yolks in a large heatproof bowl. Once the cream mixture has reached a rapid boil, remove from the heat and pour approximately 1 cup of the liquid over the yolks, whisking furiously. After the cream mixture is fully incorporated and the yolks are tempered, pour in the remaining cream mixture, whisking constantly as you do. Strain through a fine-mesh sieve into a clean container. Add the vanilla and stir to combine. Refrigerate until completely cold, then pour into an ice cream maker and freeze according to the manufacturer's directions.

Melon Sorbet

The very essence of summer, this recipe features, really, just one ingredient. It takes multiple steps to transform the melon into this dense, creamy sorbet, but don't be tempted to take shortcuts. Your reward is in the intense flavor and hue of the finished product. This is one case where you must go to the farmers' market and seek out the gnarled old guy who lovingly raises organic muskmelons—maybe Crenshaws or Hearts of Gold—and picks them only when you can smell their perfume a mile away as they warm in the sun. Go. He's there, and he'll make sure you get a good melon.

SIMPLE SYRUP

1 cup sugar

1 cup water

1 perfectly ripe, orange-fleshed melon

1/4 cup prosecco

1 lime

To make the simple syrup, combine the sugar and water in a saucepan over medium heat and heat until the sugar dissolves, stirring occasionally. Remove from the heat and allow to cool.

Halve the melon and scoop the seeds and a little pulp into a blender. Purée, then pass through a fine-mesh sieve. Place each half of the melon, cut-side down, on a cutting board and, using a sharp knife, cut down the sides to remove all trace of rind. Cut the flesh into chunks.

Clean the blender and add the purée back in, along with the melon chunks. Purée on low to avoid incorporating air into the mixture. When you have a juicy, chunky purée, pass it through a fine-mesh sieve to catch all the juice and leave the flesh behind. Place the remaining flesh in the blender for a final spin, this time processing on high. Pass this purée through the sieve as well. Place all the juice in a bowl and add the prosecco.

Add the simple syrup to taste. You may not need much, depending on the ripeness and flavor of the melon. Start in the neighborhood of 1/4 cup and go from there. Add a squeeze or two of lime juice to taste until the mixture is well balanced (start with a couple of teaspoons). Cover, place in the refrigerator, and chill until cold. Pour into an ice cream maker and freeze according to the manufacturer's directions.

Campari–Blood Orange Sorbet

Campari and soda is one of my favorite aperitifs. Not only is Campari a brilliant vermilion that looks stunning in the glass, but also the liquor's bitter edge whets the appetite for the dishes to come. Transformed into a gorgeous, not-too-sweet sorbet, Campari is equally at home finishing a meal. (Although this sorbet would also make a nice refresher between courses if you were feeling fancy.) The addition of sweet, ruby-hued blood orange juice makes this a perfect dessert for midwinter when summer's fruits are still months away. Before you freeze your sorbet, I recommend you pour a little into a highball glass and add some ice and gin. It makes the wait so much more enjoyable.

To make the simple syrup, combine the sugar, water, and orange zest in a saucepan over medium heat and heat until the sugar dissolves, stirring occasionally. Remove from the heat and allow to cool. Remove the zest before using.

Cut the oranges in half. Using a juicer or a reamer, juice the oranges and transfer the juice to a nonreactive bowl. Add the Campari. Add the simple syrup to taste, beginning with $1/3$ cup and adding additional tablespoons to taste. If you like, reserve some of the juice for your cocktail. Cover the rest of the juice and chill in the refrigerator until cold. Pour into an ice cream maker and freeze according to the manufacturer's directions.

ORANGE SIMPLE SYRUP

1 cup sugar

1 cup water

8 strips orange zest removed with a vegetable peeler

2 pounds blood oranges (should yield about 2 cups juice)

$1/4$ to $1/2$ cup Campari, to taste

Blueberry-Basil Sorbet

Although I've outed myself as someone who often prefers savory to sweet, even after dinner, I've found the perfect compromise that is sure to keep everyone happy. This is one of my favorite summer desserts, for those long, hot nights when you crave something lighter as a finish to your meal. This sorbet is just the ticket; make it when the blueberries are fat and sweet and fresh basil is everywhere you look.

3 pints fresh blueberries

3/4 cup sugar

Pinch of Kosher salt

1 teaspoon balsamic vinegar

1/2 cup water

6 sprigs basil on the stem

1/4 cup prosecco

1 tablespoon fresh lemon juice

Combine the blueberries, sugar, salt, vinegar, and water in a heatproof bowl or the top of a double boiler. Heat over simmering water for about 10 minutes, or until the berries burst and release their juices. Rub the basil stems between your fingers to release the oils and add to the berries while they are still hot. Let steep for 10 minutes.

Set aside 1 cup of poached berries to fold in at the end. Remove and discard the basil. Push the remaining berries and juice through a fine-mesh sieve. Add the prosecco, lemon juice, and reserved berries and stir to combine. Cover, place in the refrigerator, and chill until cold. Pour into an ice cream maker and freeze according to the manufacturer's directions.

Zabaglione with Mixed Berries

This is an Italian classic, with a twist. Traditionally made with Marsala, I like to vary it by using Viognier, or even prosecco, as we do here. The wine adds a dimension to the custard and marries well with the sweet berries. If you don't have a kitchen torch, skip the step where you sprinkle on the sugar and simply serve the custard spooned over the berries. If you use the broiler instead of a torch, the custard will get too soft.

1 tablespoon fresh lemon juice

$1/2$ vanilla bean, scraped

4 strips zest from 1 orange

4 strips zest from 1 lemon

11 large fresh egg yolks, at room temperature

1 cup granulated sugar

Pinch of Kosher salt

2 cups prosecco

1 tablespoon crème fraîche or sour cream

1 quart mixed fresh berries

Raw sugar, for sprinkling

Place the lemon juice, vanilla, orange and lemon zest, egg yolks, granulated sugar, salt, and wine in a heatproof bowl or the top of a double boiler and whisk to combine. Place over barely simmering water and cook, whisking constantly, for 3 to 4 minutes, or until there is no liquid in the bottom of the bowl and the mixture is completely fluffy and foamy. Remove from the heat. While still warm, fold in the crème fraîche. Place the bowl over an ice bath and chill until cold.

To serve, spoon the berries into individual ramekins or gratin dishes. Top each with a scant $1/2$ cup of zabaglione. Sprinkle with raw sugar and use a kitchen torch to caramelize the sugar. Serve immediately, while the custard is still cold.

Espresso Granita with Grappa Cream

This intensely flavored granita is the perfect answer for those who don't want to choose between a nice macchiato and a sweet finish to the meal. The Grappa Cream adds an elegant, and boozy, touch. Although it has only three ingredients, you need to plan ahead for the granita. It will take about 6 hours to freeze, and you need to fluff it with a fork every hour to ensure the texture is light.

2^1/$_2$ cups espresso diluted with 3^1/$_2$ cups cold water, or 6 cups very strong coffee

^{1}/$_2$ cup granulated sugar

^{1}/$_4$ cup packed brown sugar

Grappa Cream, for serving (recipe follows)

In a large heatproof bowl, combine the coffee and both sugars and stir until the sugars dissolve. Place the mixture in a metal container (a pie tin would work well) and put in the freezer. Stir with a fork about every hour, lifting and separating the crystals. It will take about 6 hours to freeze completely. Scoop into stemmed glass bowls or martini glasses and serve with the Grappa Cream.

GRAPPA CREAM

1^1/$_2$ cups heavy cream

3 tablespoons sugar

Pinch of Kosher salt

^{1}/$_4$ cup grappa

Whip the cream until well thickened but not airy. Add the sugar and salt and whisk to incorporate completely. Add the grappa and whisk to combine.

Pie Cookies

If you have a mom or grandmother who baked when you were a kid, this not-too-sweet dessert should ring the bells of nostalgia for you. A cookie designed to emulate those cinnamon-and-sugared scraps of leftover pie dough, these pretty pinwheels can cozy up quite happily to a cup of tea, or would make a welcome finishing touch to an evening espresso.

DOUGH

2 cups all-purpose flour, plus more for sprinkling

¹/₂ teaspoon kosher salt

2 teaspoons granulated sugar

¹/₂ cup cold unsalted butter

¹/₄ cup ice water

FILLING

4 tablespoons unsalted butter, softened

2 tablespoons granulated sugar

1 tablespoon ground cinnamon

¹/₈ teaspoon Kosher salt

1 fresh egg, beaten, for egg wash

Turbinado sugar, for sprinkling

To make the dough, combine the flour, salt, granulated sugar, and butter in a food processor and pulse until completely blended and the mixture is fine and sandy. Add the ice water, 1 tablespoon at a time, until the mixture forms clumps the size of gravel or small stones and the dough holds together when you squeeze it. Place the dough on a lightly floured board and form into a disk. Knead the dough, smearing it across the board with the heel of your hand 4 or 5 times, until the mixture just comes together and forms a smooth dough. Do not over-knead. Gather again into a disk, wrap well, and chill for 1 hour.

To make the filling, combine all the ingredients and blend well with a fork.

Once the dough has chilled, lay out a piece of parchment and sprinkle it with flour. Rub your rolling pin with flour as well. Roll out the dough into a square or rectangular shape (do the best you can) about ¹/₈ inch thick. Using an offset spatula, spread the filling in a very thin layer over the dough, leaving a 1-inch border on all sides. Brush the borders with the beaten egg. Roll the dough up tightly along one long edge, pressing down to seal. You should end up with an 18-inch log. Roll up in parchment and place in the fridge to chill for 30 minutes.

Preheat the oven to 450°F.

Brush the log with the remaining egg wash, then cut into 1-inch slices. Place the slices flat on a parchment-lined baking sheet and sprinkle the cut sides liberally with turbinado sugar. Bake for 10 minutes, then decrease the heat to 325°F and bake for 15 minutes longer, or until lightly browned and puffed. Transfer to a wire rack to cool.

Cardamom Sablés

Cardamom is used everywhere from India to Scandinavia, and I love what the fragrant spice does for these classic French shortbread cookies. Though not traditional, the addition of cornstarch guarantees the delicate, crumbly texture for which the cookies are named (*sablé* translates as "sand"). Because sablés need time to chill before being baked, they make wonderful icebox cookies and are easy to keep in the fridge or the freezer and you can slice and bake as needed. They make an easy but distinctive finish to a meal, and are a nice accessory for a lonely scoop of ice cream or sorbet. If you like, instead of forming the dough into logs, roll out the dough after chilling and cut out rounds, then baked as directed. Cardamom loses its fragrance quickly, so make sure your ground cardamom is fresh.

1 cup unsalted butter, softened

¹/₂ cup sugar

1¹/₂ teaspoons ground cardamom

2 tablespoons cornstarch

¹/₂ teaspoon Kosher salt

2 cups all-purpose flour

Using the paddle attachment of your stand mixer, combine the butter, sugar, and cardamom on medium-high speed. Add the cornstarch and salt and mix to blend. Add the flour and mix on low just until combined. Divide the dough into 2 logs, about 2 inches in diameter, and wrap each tightly in plastic wrap. Chill for at least 1 hour, or until the dough is firm.

When ready to bake, preheat the oven to 350°F. Line 2 baking sheets with parchment paper.

Slice the logs crosswise into ¹/₄-inch-thick coins and place on the prepared baking sheets. Bake for 12 to 15 minutes, or until the sablés are lightly browned around the edges. Let cool for a couple of minutes on the sheets, then transfer to a wire rack to cool completely. The cookies will keep for about a week in an airtight container.

Almond Cake with Bay-Poached Queen Anne Cherries

MAKES ONE 9-INCH CAKE OR 8 INDIVIDUAL SERVINGS

If the combination of olive oil and dessert falls outside your comfort zone, I guarantee this cake will make you a total convert. This luscious specimen has the richness of a traditional pound cake but a more complex texture, all complemented by the haunting fruitiness of extra-virgin olive oil. Almond meal, or almonds ground until fine, gives it a delicate nuttiness. Completely addictive on its own, this cake is even better dressed up with fresh spring cherries scented with fresh bay and a tangy dollop of crème fraîche. These pretty, yellow- and pink-hued cherries are more commonly known as Rainiers, but I like this moniker better because one of the restaurants sits perched atop Seattle's Queen Anne Hill. It's essential to use fresh bay leaves in this recipe. Dried bay is too strong and will give the cherries an almost medicinal taste, not a quality I look for in a dessert.

1/2 cup extra-virgin olive oil

1/2 cup unsalted butter, softened

1 teaspoon kosher salt

1 1/4 cups sugar

Pinch of nutmeg

4 large fresh eggs

Zest of 1 lemon

4 teaspoons fresh lemon juice

1/4 teaspoon pure vanilla extract

1 cup almond meal

2/3 cup all-purpose flour

Bay-Poached Queen Anne Cherries, for accompaniment (recipe follows)

Crème fraîche, for serving

Preheat the oven to 350°F. Butter the bottom and sides of a 9-inch cake pan or 8 6-ounce ramekins and set aside.

In a stand mixer, or in a large bowl if using a hand mixer, cream together the olive oil, butter, salt, and sugar. When well combined, add a pinch of nutmeg, about 5 swipes of a whole nutmeg on a grater. Continue to beat on high speed until the mixture lightens nearly to white and almost doubles in size. It should almost resemble a meringue in texture at this point. Scrape down the bowl. With the mixer on medium speed, add the eggs one at a time.

Add the lemon zest, lemon juice, vanilla, and almond meal and mix to combine. Add the flour and beat just until incorporated.

Pour the batter into the prepared pan or divide among the ramekins and place on the center rack in the oven. Bake for 1 hour, or until a knife inserted into the center comes out completely clean. For the ramekins, bake for 20 to 30 minutes, or until a skewer inserted in the center comes out clean. Allow to cool in the pan set on a wire rack. When the cake is completely cool, run a sharp knife around the perimeter of the cake and turn out onto a platter or cake plate. Serve with the bay-poached cherries and a dollop of crème fraîche.

continued

BAY-POACHED QUEEN ANNE CHERRIES

1 quart Queen Anne or Rainier cherries, pitted and halved

$1/2$ cup sugar

Pinch of Kosher salt

2 fresh bay leaves, torn in half

$1/4$ cup white wine

Combine the cherries, sugar, salt, and bay leaves in a bowl and allow to macerate for at least 30 minutes, or until the juices begin to come out of the cherries.

Place the mixture in the top of a double boiler or heatproof bowl and set over gently simmering water. Add the wine and stir to combine. Cook for 10 minutes, or until the cherries soften and the liquid becomes thick and syrupy. Remove from the heat and allow the cherries to cool in their liquid. Serve with almond cake and crème fraîche.

Pine Nut Crumbles

I love how Italians use nuts in desserts, from almond cake to pine nut tarts. Here, those same pine nuts transform the humble cookie into something truly special. Crumbly, yes, but not too sweet—just delicate and fabulous. For a variation, try filling the thumbprints with homemade jam. Rhubarb would be delicious, making each cookie taste a little like PB&J.

2 cups pine nuts, lightly toasted

$1/2$ teaspoon ground cinnamon

1 cup turbinado sugar

$1^1/4$ cups all-purpose flour

$1/2$ cup unsalted butter

$3/4$ teaspoon Kosher salt

Preheat the oven to 325°F.

Place the pine nuts in a food processor fitted with the metal blade and process until coarsely ground. Remove half of the nuts to a bowl and reserve. Add the cinnamon and sugar to the remaining nuts in the bowl of the processor and continue to process until finely ground, about the texture of cornmeal. Add the flour and process until combined. Add the mixture to the reserved pine nuts and toss to combine.

Melt the butter in a small saucepan over low heat. Pour the hot butter over the pine nut mixture and work in with a spatula. Sprinkle the salt over and work in. Pinch off pieces about the size of 2 tablespoons, roll into balls, then flatten slightly. Put a cute dimple in the top of each with your thumb. Place $1/2$ inch apart on a parchment-lined baking sheet.

Bake on the center rack of the oven for 45 minutes to 1 hour, or until firm and lightly browned. Transfer to a wire rack to cool.

Chocolate Pumpkin Tart

They say that pumpkin pie is one of the scents that men react to most strongly. I'm not sure if I agree, but I think that by combining a smooth pumpkin filling with a chocolate crust, you have a good chance of getting your guests' attention. I roast the pumpkin in the oven to ensure the filling isn't watery. It's really not possible to overcook the pumpkin; in fact, the longer you cook it, the more the flavors become concentrated. If you can't find a sugar pumpkin, butternut squash or another hard-skinned fall squash would make a fine substitute. You can roast the pumpkin and bake the crusts at the same time, speeding the process along.

CRUST

$1/2$ cup sugar

1 cup pistachios, toasted

4 tablespoons cocoa powder

1 cup all-purpose flour

$1/2$ teaspoon kosher salt

6 tablespoons unsalted butter

FILLING

6 tablespoons unsalted butter

1 small sugar pumpkin or butternut squash (about $2 1/2$ pounds), peeled and diced

4 tablespoons dark rum

7 fresh egg yolks

$3/4$ cup firmly packed dark brown sugar

$3/4$ cup crème fraîche

$1/4$ cup maple syrup

$1/4$ cup all-purpose flour

2 teaspoons ground cinnamon

2 teaspoons ground ginger

$1/2$ teaspoon ground nutmeg

1 teaspoon ground allspice

$1/4$ teaspoon ground clove

$1/2$ teaspoon kosher salt, plus extra for roasting

2 teaspoons pure vanilla extract

1 teaspoon lemon juice

1 cup chopped chocolate or chocolate chips

1 tablespoon corn syrup

Preheat the oven to 325°F.

To make the crust, place the sugar and pistachios in the bowl of a food processor and pulverize until the nuts are coarsely ground. Remove half the nuts and reserve, then continue to process the remaining nuts and sugar until the mixture is finely ground and sandy. Add the cocoa powder, flour, salt, and butter and pulse until combined. Add the reserved nuts back in and pulse two or three times. Divide the mixture, and pat into the bottom of two 9-inch tart pans. Bake for 35 to 40 minutes, or until firm. Allow to cool on a wire rack for about 20 minutes.

Increase the oven temperature to 350°F.

To make the filling, melt the butter with a pinch of salt in a small saucepan over low heat, then toss with the diced pumpkin in a bowl. Spread out on a baking sheet and roast for 20 to 25 minutes, or until completely soft. Scrape the pumpkin mixture into a blender and purée until smooth. Pour into a bowl and allow to cool to at least room temperature; you can put the mixture in the fridge to hurry things along if you like. If you want the texture perfectly silky, pass through a tamis or other fine-mesh sieve. Measure out $1^1/_2$ cups of the purée and whisk in the rum, egg yolks, brown sugar, crème fraîche, maple syrup, flour, cinnamon, ginger, and nutmeg, allspice, clove, salt, vanilla, and lemon juice. Reserve.

Decrease the oven temperature to 300°F.

Combine the chocolate and corn syrup in a double boiler and melt over medium heat. Divide the mixture in half, then spread over the cooled crusts, leaving a $^1/_2$-inch border all the way around the edges to prevent the chocolate from burning.

Place the tart pans on baking sheets. Divide the pumpkin mixture in half, then pour over the chocolate on each tart and smooth the tops. Bake for 45 minutes to 1 hour (rotate the baking sheets after 30 minutes), or until the centers are set.

Building Blocks: Condiments, Sauces, and Staples

One of the not-so-secret secrets about restaurants is that we keep "fancy" staples on hand, making it easier to whip up an interesting, perhaps more complex, dish on a busy line. The same principle works just as well at home for cut-above cooking on a whim. You can make bruschetta or fry up some clams without a tangy homemade aioli as an accent, but using it puts the dish over the top. We've all had soup or a chopped salad made with canned chickpeas. Make a batch of your own using basic aromatics and it will prove a revelation for you—the delicate, nutty flavor and creamy texture so unlike what you're used to. And while there are plenty of recipes in this book that use dried pasta, there are none that use jarred tomato sauce. You can guess the reason for that. But again, making your own doesn't take much time, offers incomparable flavor, and helps make a host of dishes special. Use the recipes in this section to build your own layers of flavor. I'll keep your secret.

Basic Tomato Sauce

If you master any one recipe in this book, this should be it. Not only does a bright, fresh tomato sauce turn any freshly made pasta into an event, but it's also an indispensable component in dishes from basic ragus to Maloreddus with Squid, Tomato Sauce, and Lemon (page 97) and Linguine with Shrimp (page 90). Part of the fun of making your own sauce is squishing the whole tomatoes—and they must be San Marzanos—with your fingers. It can get messy, especially for those of us who wear glasses, but it's worth it (and a good stress-reduction technique, to boot). Find an apron and get ready for a simple, well-balanced sauce that you'll always want to have on hand. And when you can have this sauce ready in under an hour, why ever open a jar again?

2 (28-ounce) cans whole, peeled San Marzano tomatoes

1/4 cup extra-virgin olive oil

2 onions, finely chopped

6 cloves garlic, sliced

8 to 10 fresh basil leaves, depending on size

Kosher salt and freshly ground pepper

Put the tomatoes in a deep bowl and crush them with your fingers. Heat the olive oil in a large saucepan over medium heat and sauté the onions and garlic until tender but not browned, 5 to 6 minutes. Add the tomatoes and basil leaves. Cook over medium-low heat for 30 to 40 minutes. Season lightly with salt and pepper.

Use an immersion blender, if you have one, or pulse in a food processor to create a rough purée with some texture. The sauce keeps, covered, in the fridge for up to 3 days and freezes well.

SAN MARZANO TOMATOES

San Marzanos are the "it" tomatoes these days. You'll hear lots of chefs wax poetic about the volcanic soil in which they're grown, in an area close to Naples, or about their distinguished pedigree going back hundreds of years. For me, it boils down to meaty flesh—much, much more flesh to water as compared to regular plum tomatoes—and a sweet flavor that makes a difference you can really taste. Whether or not you buy the romantic backstory, make sure you use them in your sauce. Several imported brands are readily available in most markets these days.

Mayonnaise

Mayonnaise has an undeserved reputation for being difficult to make. With an egg yolk and some mustard as binders, and the help of a food processor when adding the oil, homemade mayo is as easy to make as it is delicious.

1 fresh egg yolk

2 tablespoons water

1 teaspoon Dijon mustard

Juice of ¹/₂ lemon

1¹/₂ cups canola oil or other mild-flavored oil

Kosher salt

Put the egg yolk, water, mustard, and lemon juice in the bowl of a food processor and pulse to combine. With the motor running, add the oil through the feed tube in a slow but steady stream and process until a smooth mayonnaise forms. Season to taste with salt. It will keep for two days in the refrigerator.

VARIATION: SPRING GARLIC AIOLI

Follow the mayonnaise recipe above, adding 1 stalk chopped spring garlic. Strain the aioli through a sieve to catch any tough fibers.

Preserved Garlic

The delicate, herbaceous quality of preserved garlic adds a bit of bite where raw garlic would be too harsh and overwhelm more subtle flavors, such as the lobster mushroom recipe on page 119. Make sure you use a peeler to zest the lemon. Using a grater or Microplane would release too many oils and create too strong a flavor. As a bonus, use the oil in vinaigrettes or drizzle on grilled fish.

1 lemon

1 head garlic, peeled (12 to 15 cloves)

3 sprigs thyme

1 cup extra-virgin olive oil

Using a vegetable peeler, remove half of the lemon peel, about 3 or 4 large long strips in all. Place in a saucepan with the garlic cloves, thyme, and oil. Place over low heat and keep at a bare simmer until the garlic is tender when pierced with the tip of a knife, 20 to 25 minutes. Pour into a glass jar with a lid. The garlic can be used immediately or will keep, refrigerated, for up to 2 weeks.

Preserved Lemons

AS DESIRED

Italians don't use preserved lemons—they're more of a Moroccan thing. But more lemons come out of Sicily than anywhere else, and the intense, concentrated flavor of preserved lemon peel is perfect in dishes such as Grilled Mackerel with Crispy Potatoes and Caper and Preserved Lemon Sauce (page 181). You'll need a large sterilized jar with a lid for this recipe.

Organic or unsprayed lemons
Kosher salt

Wash the lemons and carefully dry them. Cut lengthwise into quarters, keeping them intact at one end. They should look a bit like flowers.

Pour a 1-inch layer of salt in the bottom of the jar. Add a layer of lemons and top with salt. Repeat the salt and lemon layering process almost to the top of the jar, ending with salt. Pop into the fridge. In a day or so the lemons will release their juice and produce liquid. When this happens, pour in additional salt to cover.

When you want to use the lemons, remove what you need and thoroughly rinse off the salt. Using a sharp knife, cut off any flesh and discard. Use the rind as called for in the recipe. Keep the remaining lemons in the jar, adding additional salt as needed to keep them covered. Preserved lemons will keep indefinitely in the refrigerator.

Preserved Pecorino Sardo

MAKES 1 POUND

This is less a recipe than an idea, but I assure you that it's an idea that will continue to inspire you. It began with a jar of marinated Sardinian pecorino that I bought and kept at one of the restaurants. Although the price of the cheese made it as precious as gold, I soon found that it enhanced nearly everything it touched, from pastas to carpaccios. (I admit it's also terrific snitched directly out of the jar.) If kept covered in olive oil, the cheese will keep nearly indefinitely, though it's so irrisistable that it won't last that long. Make sure it is allowed to come to room temperature before using. As you use up the cheese, add the olive oil to vinaigrettes, pasta, and more.

1 pound young (fresh) Pecorino Sardo
Extra-virgin olive oil

Cut the rind from the cheese, then cut the cheese into 1-inch cubes and pack into a sterilized jar. Add oil to cover completely (the amount of oil will depend on the shape of your jar). Allow to marinate for at least a day or two before using. Covered in oil, the cheese will keep indefinitely in the refrigerator. Make sure that you always remove cheese using clean utensils, and not your fingers.

Salsa Verde

This kicky sauce is matched in flavor by its dramatic green color. Bright with parsley and with deep notes from the anchovy, salsa verde makes plain grilled fish or meat into something you want to serve to company, and it adds an herby note to rich organ meats or tongue. Try adding a spoonful to soups or tossing with plain boiled potatoes.

1 bunch parsley

1 lemon

6 anchovy fillets

Kosher salt and freshly cracked pepper

$^1/_2$ cup extra-virgin olive oil

Wash and dry the parsley, then remove all the leaves from the stems. Using a vegetable peeler, remove half of the lemon peel in 3 or 4 large strips. Place the lemon peel and parsley in a food processor with the anchovies, a pinch of salt, and some freshly cracked pepper. Pulse to combine. With the motor running, add the olive oil in a steady stream and blend for 1 to 2 minutes, until you have a chunky, thick green purée. This is best used right away, but will keep for up to 2 days in the fridge, covered.

VARIATION: PINE-NUT SALSA VERDE

Add $^1/_4$ cup toasted pine nuts to the food processor after pulsing the parsley, lemon peel, anchovies, salt, and pepper, but before adding the oil. Continue with recipe as directed.

Garlic Breadcrumbs

You can customize these crumbs with lemon zest, oregano, parsley, or other herbs. Simply reprocess the crumbs with the herbs after you have finished the basic recipe. They have a thousand uses, and are excellent as a topping for oysters, artichokes, pastas, and more.

1 pound stale bread, sliced

$1/4$ cup extra-virgin olive oil

2 cloves garlic, smashed with a knife

Kosher salt

Preheat the oven to 350°F.

Place the bread slices on a baking sheet and bake until lightly toasted and dry, 10 to 12 minutes. While the bread toasts, place the olive oil and garlic in a sauté pan and set over low heat. Cook gently, allowing the garlic to infuse the oil.

When the bread slices are toasted, place in a food processor and pulse until finely ground. Add the crumbs to the garlic oil and stir gently until coated. Season to taste with salt and cook for 2 to 3 minutes, or until the oil is absorbed. Remove the garlic cloves. The crumbs will keep in an airtight container at room temperature for about 2 weeks.

Basic Chickpeas

This great staple forms the basis for other delicious dishes, including the Mediterranean Mussel and Chickpea Soup with Fennel and Lemon (page 44), and can be used in salads and purées. The simple preparation will win you over to ditching the can and cooking your own, allowing you to fully appreciate the delicate nuttiness and incomparable texture.

1 cup dried chickpeas, soaked overnight in water to cover

$1/2$ small carrot, peeled and halved lengthwise

1 stalk celery

3 cloves garlic

$1/2$ small onion, peeled

Drain the soaking liquid from the chickpeas and place them in a saucepan with the carrot, celery, garlic, and onion. Cover with water by 2 inches and bring to a boil. Decrease the heat to maintain a bare simmer and cook until tender, 45 minutes to 1 hour. When the chickpeas are tender, drain and use immediately, discarding the other vegetables; or if you won't be using them right away, transfer them and their cooking liquid to a container and store in the refrigerator for up to 4 days.

Index

MEASUREMENT CONVERSION CHARTS

VOLUME

U.S.	Imperial	Metric
1 tablespoon	1/2 fl oz	15 ml
2 tablespoons	1 fl oz	30 ml
1/4 cup	2 fl oz	60 ml
1/3 cup	3 fl oz	90 ml
1/2 cup	4 fl oz	120 ml
2/3 cup	5 fl oz (1/4 pint)	150 ml
3/4 cup	6 fl oz	180 ml
1 cup	8 fl oz (1/3 pint)	240 ml
1 1/4 cups	10 fl oz (1/2 pint)	300 ml
2 cups (1 pint)	16 fl oz (2/3 pint)	480 ml
2 1/2 cups	20 fl oz (1 pint)	600 ml
1 quart	32 fl oz (1 2/3 pint)	1 l

TEMPERATURE

Fahrenheit	Celsius/Gas Mark
250°F	120°C/gas mark 1/2
275°F	135°C/gas mark 1
300°F	150°C/gas mark 2
325°F	160°C/gas mark 3
350°F	180 or 175°C/gas mark 4
375°F	190°C/gas mark 5
400°F	200°C/gas mark 6
425°F	220°C/gas mark 7
450°F	230°C/gas mark 8
475°F	245°C/gas mark 9
500°F	260°C

LENGTH

Inch	Metric
1/4 inch	6 mm
1/2 inch	1.25 cm
3/4 inch	2 cm
1 inch	2.5 cm
6 inches (1/2 foot)	15 cm
12 inches (1 foot)	30 cm

WEIGHT

U.S./Imperial	Metric
1/2 oz	15 g
1 oz	30 g
2 oz	60 g
1/4 lb	115 g
1/3 lb	150 g
1/2 lb	225 g
3/4 lb	350 g
1 lb	450 g